I0438259

THE
WORKING
MAN
FIGHTS
FOR RIGHT

TAMING A DICTATING GOVERNMENT

Scott Jeffrey Filip

Copyright © 2013 by Scott Jeffrey Filip

Published by Dusty Road Press
www.glcpress.com
All rights reserved by the author.

10 9 8 7 6 5 4 3 2 1   FIRST EDITION

Publisher's Note:

This is a political work that is based upon the opinions of the author. The written contents of this book are not intended to encourage any violent acts against any representative or official of the United States government, either appointed or elected, nor does it condone the overthrow of the duly elected representatives of the United States government. The author believes in freedom of speech as stated in the first amendment of the United States Constitution and is merely exercising that right as expressed within the pages of this written work.

LIBRARY OF CONGRESS CATALOGING-IN-PUBLICATION DATA
Filip, Scott Jeffrey.
The Working Man Fights for Right / Scott Jeffrey Filip
p. cm.

ISBN-13: 978-1500114480   ISBN-10: 1500114480

1. United States Government—Non Fiction. 2. Barack Obama—Opinion/Non Fiction. 3. Current American Lifestyles—Non Fiction.
4. Right Wing Philosophies—Non Fiction. 5. Texas Authors
I. Title

Printed in the United States of America
Set in **Palatino Linotype**
Book Designed by Lee McCain
Cover Designed by Nancy McGee

Without limiting the rights under copyright reserved above, no part of this publication may be reproduced, stored in or introduced into a retrieval system, or transmitted, in any form or by any means (electronic, mechanical, photocopying, recording, or otherwise), without the prior written permission of both the copyright owner and the above publisher of this book.

The scanning, uploading, and distribution of this book via the Internet or via any other means without the permission of the publisher is illegal and punishable by law. Please purchase only authorized electronic editions, and do not participate in or encourage piracy of copyrightable materials. Your support of the author's rights is greatly appreciated.

This book — inspired by my wife and children — is dedicated to the working class, the entrepreneurs, and to our service men and women across the United States of America. Thank you.

CONTENTS

THE WORKING MAN FIGHTS FOR RIGHT

TAMING A DICTATING GOVERNMENT

"I predict future happiness for Americans, if they can prevent the government from wasting the labors of the people under the pretense of taking care of them."

— Thomas Jefferson

INTRODUCTION

Hello, America! How are you? This is the Working Man talking to you today and I am willing to bet you feel the same way I do. We all wanted change didn't we? Well, maybe some did, right? I have some questions throughout the book that may give you pause. Of course it depends on how you feel about the situation, or perhaps the mood you are in as you turn these pages.

✑

America, I am just a simple man minding my own business and do so without bothering everyone around me. I love helping people out and you don't have to pay me for helping you for every little thing. Helping people and getting a thank you or a hug, or maybe a simple hand shake, is worth more than any paycheck to me.

The best thing about me is that I am an American. I am free and plan to stay that way. I pray every day that God protects me, my family, Texas, and my country. We live in the best country in the world. God created America and now it is up to us to maintain a wealthy nation. Keep God first in your life and you will be the person you never thought you would or could be.

One other thing I've discovered as I get older is that I also love to motivate people. There are a lot of things that bring us down in the world but we have to have a mindset to succeed and not just settle for getting by or just saying that something is good enough. You need to settle for nothing but the best. The sky truly is the limit.

I am from a small town in south Texas. No fancy car or truck. No big mansion on a hill. Just a regular guy worried about the best country in the world, these United States of America.

Look around you, opportunity is right under your nose. What is freedom to you? For me, freedom is having the individual strength to build a business as big

The Working Man Fights for Right

as I want. It represents my choice to choose an insurance plan that I want. Freedom to me is walking outside my home and going to work without worrying about some bomb going off on a street I drive down every day. Freedom to me is having the right to speak out and then not get shouted down for it; in other words, freedom of speech.

True America is a place where you can go hunting or fishing with your gun and not worry about it being taken away from you. And to pick any lake or river or coastline to throw out a line to bring home supper.

Freedom is when you can go watch your son play a football game on a Thursday or Friday night. To see him play baseball, soccer, or basketball is everything to a true American. For a father to go visit his son or daughter in the military for a couple of weeks while they are on leave.

Freedom is my truck that I drive, for however long I wish, and to use as much fuel as I want in the process. To order any kind of food that I want to eat, and to eat as much as I want is freedom.

Freedom is me worshipping at any church I choose. Freedom is to be with my family until the day I die and not have somebody try and tell me any different.

Freedom is to vote a candidate in to office and to flush him out if he doesn't live up to my expectations.

෨

Freedom is to have the right to privacy. The right to bear arms and to protect myself, and my property, so help me God. To choose what I want to do with my own life and not let anyone tell me that I can't. To have a conservative movement like no other movement in history.

We live in the greatest country in the world. We all know this. We all believe this. We all breathe this. And we will all die living the freedoms of an American. We cannot let corruption invade our lives. We must not let the devil destroy the country we dearly love. Allow God to stay within us at all times. Give our military personnel the strength and guidance that they need. Protect them each and every day while they fight the enemy for freedom; for them, and also for us.

Freedom is watching the sun go down with the one you love the most. Freedom is waking up in the morning with your kids snuggled up beside you on a cold and rainy morning.

Freedom is being in the Tea Party and being free to protest the bills and programs that are destroying our country. Our gatherings across the country are true historical moments in our country. The people of our country, *are* the country. Our country is the working class, the entrepreneur, and our service men and women. That is freedom to me.

The Working Man Fights for Right

I won't go into detail about not having freedom. You know what you may lose in the days to come. You know that our liberties are at stake here. You know your kids' lives have some major challenges ahead that we have not even experienced ourselves because these are problems we couldn't have ever imagined when we were their age.

You know that where this country is going is not the America that you want. Whether you are a conservative or even a liberal, we all live in the same country together. And we need to wake up and smell the coffee. God is watching over us every day. So we need to show him that we do care about our great land. We have a duty. And that duty is to keep and maintain the very same country that God gave us all those long years ago. This is the home of the brave and the land of the free. Yes, the land of the *free*.

Have you forgotten September 11, 2001? What happened on 9/11? The planes got hijacked and our country was changed forever. How did that make you feel? Just read some more and you will know how I felt.

Picture 9/11 in your mind. I was angry, hurt, sad, and confused, all at the same time. So overall I can't say that I know how I really felt.

ॐ

What was your reaction after the Pentagon was hit? What about the World Trade Center, or the plane crashing in the field? The buildings crumbling down around the firefighters and police after they went in was a heart wrenching sight to see. So with that being said, I haven't forgotten about that September day.

Let me refresh your memory. American Airlines flight 11, a Boeing 767, had 92 passengers on it. The plane departed at 8 o'clock in the morning from Boston Logan International Airport. Their journey was sadly shortened. That plane hit the North Tower at 8:45 a.m. and the tower later collapsed at 10:28 a.m.

The second plane that was sadly taken from us with 65 passengers was another Boeing 767, United flight 175. It also left Boston around the same time at the American flight. This one went for the South tower at 9:03 a.m., and the building fell at 10:05 a.m.

Flight 77 was an American Airlines Boeing 757 with 64 passengers aboard. This one departed at 8:21 a.m. from Dulles Airport in Washington D.C. The crash happened at the west wall of the Pentagon at 9:45 a.m. It is believed that this flight was meant for the Capitol building.

And the last doomed airliner changed our lives forever. Flight 93, United Airlines Boeing 757 with 45 passengers aboard left Newark, New Jersey at 8:43 a.m.

The Working Man Fights for Right

◆

Heroic efforts to take back the plane from the Muslim terrorists were made by the passengers, but tragically the plane went down at 10:10 a.m. in a field southeast of Pittsburgh.

We cannot forget who we are as Americans. We cannot let this happen again. Some are resigned that it will happen again, that it's just a matter of time. I say, if we keep cutting our military defenses and fail to keep our priorities straight then yes, it may happen again.

Makes you wonder what Washington is doing, doesn't it? These are terrorists we are dealing with here. These people have no care in the world about American lives and now Washington is wanting to cut our own military defenses.

Do you remember on September 11, when George W. Bush said, "We will rid the world of these evil doers." Do you feel that way now? Do we have the momentum we had on that day of terror?

America, please wake up and smell the smoke from the burning buildings and those planes again, because times are changing on our own soil and abroad. Is it just me, or is something terribly wrong here?

The courage and the bravery exhibited by our citizens, firefighters, policeman and any others that played a role in the rescue efforts deserve more than our

ॐ

thanks. These are the true American heroes. That day is as clear in my mind as the moment it happened.

The darkness covered the city. Our world was torn apart, not just in New York, but all around the world. God help us all.

I hugged my wife and kids and stayed glued to the television set, for I don't know how long. We should not ever forget 9/11.

Do you remember when Alan Jackson's hit country song, *Where Were You When The World Stopped Turning,* played for the first time? I have a question about January 20, 2009. Where were you when the world started spinning?

It's about one o'clock in the morning and everyone is asleep; my wife, my son, and my baby daughter. While my wonderful family sleeps, daddy is still up thinking about everything around him. My wife chuckles sometimes, "When are you going to get some rest and go to sleep?"

"I can sleep when I'm dead," I smile.

My two little wiener dogs even give me bemused looks at this late hour. I guess they need their rest, too.

What is happening to America? Are you in a financial situation that is going south? Is your job in jeopardy of being eliminated? Well, I understand your

❧

feelings. I check my wallet often to see if I have enough cash to make it until my next paycheck. Things are moving way to fast and I feel it's time to speak out. A lot of people have already, but this working man is going to let America know that this is the time to get involved with politics more than ever. I am a small business owner and have a lot on my plate; juggling three or four things at once is not to easy some days.

The new power grab we now see in our political world is pretty scary to the average man or woman. Like myself, people are just trying to make ends meet while losing their retirement plans or just getting one last check after thirty or thirty-five years at one company. It's enough to make you break down and cry. I used to have one boss at my job but now it seems like I have a number of people looking over my shoulder, and in reality they are not even at my job.

Most employees these days are depressed, stressed , or downright angry. The government we have now knows it, too.

Together we'll tackle these issues throughout the book and as you'll soon see, sometimes I get pretty mad and sometimes I get pretty down. A lot of people these days are just as confused as to what to do with their lives.

~

- Should I send my kids to college?
- Should we wait to buy a new car ?
- Should we go ahead and invest some more money in the stock market or real estate?

These questions go on and on.

I am a proud Texan and proud to be an American. We are all Americans. We are a strong people. And in this book I promise to be blunt with you and straight forward because as Americans we need to know the truth.

The government likes people like us because we make the government rich. We work our butts off and seldom seem to catch get break. The more you make, the more they take. And though we can become very rich here in the USA, doesn't it seem like the government never get enough of our money?

The government also intensely dislikes people like us because we dare to question what is going on around us. They know that we're all not sheep; they know that many of us—folks like you and me—are on to their tricks, and they don't like it one little bit.

As business owners and working folk we are always trying to find better and easier ways of making money, and in many cases some people may just be missing that one little thing that will get them over that financial hump. Sounds like you, right? But we can't ever give up, in spite of Uncle Sam's greedy little hand that is always in the background.

We are entering uncharted waters here in America. That's why some nights I am up to God knows when thinking on this. We are still free but how long is that going to last? Truly. This is why we need to be involved in politics more than ever; that is a good thing.

We, the people, need to become more familiar with our surroundings and where our country is going. We are fast entering into a controlled environment and the free-minded individual is aware of this and does not like it one bit. People watch the news more than ever and that's great, but we have to learn about our leaders and try to figure out their intentions before it is too late.

The people of this country know what is going on now, and though some say it's too late to get it back, I think it's just the right time to step up and—to use a Texas saying—take the bull by the horns. Let's get to the bottom of things and let's start with Washington D.C. .

The working man is angry, and the working man is not stupid like Big Government thinks we are. We are the life blood of this country and without us Washington is nothing.

~

As the days pass I get more and more passionate about my country. The working man is tired of being run over in this country. But people are starting to wake up, as demonstrated in the 2012 national election. Yes, Mr. Obama won his second term, but even he must concede the fact that forty-six percent of a nation of 400 million did not cast a vote in his favor.

My family depends on me. If I fail, my family fails. And if that were to happen I do not believe it is my right to take the rest of the nation down with me, either. The redistribution of wealth is getting old in my eyes and it is not American. The government has more money than they know what to do with, but they will never admit that. And their key to amassing more and more is to simply tax every possible thing in the world that a working man needs to have a life here in America.

I drive a tractor trailer for a living, and boy do I see a lot of things out on the road. (Not what some of you are thinking, that's a whole other book!)

I see businesses shut down and homes for sale, most of which came on the market through foreclosure. Car dealer lots are vacant and even the traditional oil fields are slowing down to. What is going on? The bad part of it all is that some of these companies were profitable and were continuing to be, but not anymore. This is because whoever makes profits now are not friends of our current government and administration.

The working man is working overtime and our president, Barack Obama, is loving every minute of it because now he has free reign to take from the achiever and pass the wealth out to the ones who are not earning it. And you wonder why I am up after one o'clock in the morning?

Our lives are changing and we are losing personal control of them every day. People are working so hard now that they are losing sleep, working longer hours, and are forced to be away from their families more.

Some people used to say, "Take this job and shove it!" Now they are saying, "I'll keep this job, I love it."

Once you read this book become another voice for America because she needs the individual now more than ever. We need common sense people back in Washington and we need them soon.

Be motivated to not be silenced anymore. Remember, you are not alone. The working man has a lot to be proud of and we will not lose everything we have worked for to someone who likes to spread your wealth and give it to someone else who is too lazy to work on their own. We live in the land of opportunity but many have just have not realized it yet.

❧

We have three challenges we face today for those of you who want to continue to have true Freedom in your lives.

The first one is that our government loves nothing better than a financial foreign policy crisis.

The second is that some want unions such as the Teamsters and the SEIU, and social organizers like ACORN. The only thing that these groups want is money and power.

The third is the redistribution of wealth. They want to return our wealth "to its rightful owners." When I say our wealth, I am talking about the working people of America. And who are the "rightful owners?" The people who do not lift a finger to do anything in their lives except to expect others to take care of them. This isn't only about your freedom, America, it is about money and power. And who is going to pay for all of this corruption? The American tax payer. And who are the tax payers? Look in the mirror.

There was a time when many Americans wanted more government in their lives but now some regret it. A salesman sells things for a purpose and so does a politician. To make money and to gain power.

Some salesman will take you for everything you've got. This is what we have now:

ৎ

- Innocent people are losing their lifelong businesses and investments. I know some things were going on before 2008, but what is going on now needs to be stopped, and stopped soon.

- Government stimulus packages are not the answer. Businesses need to restructure on their own. There will be job losses, so why hype up government when we are losing jobs anyway?

- If you are not in a union, you are disliked. If you are not on President Obama's side you are not in a good position. When Obama says he wants to help all Americans that, to me, is not true. He will help some, but at the same time destroy others in the process.

We have a nation of great people and stability and we need those people back in Washington.

The President preaches about equality for America and of being united. But this country seems to be more divided than ever. We need to spread the good news of this great country, not tear it down just to be like everyone else.

❧

When I was a young lad, I really didn't think about my world around me or what I was really going to do with my life. I was basically happy just being a kid, sometimes having fun and sometimes getting my butt chewed out by my parents.

I would come home from school and I would play or do my homework. At 5:10 p.m. on the dot my dear old dad would pull into the driveway and I would start bugging him to throw ball with me. Or maybe even get him to help me with my homework.

My dad would kiss mom then he would make his way to the refrigerator and grab an ice cold beer and turn on the T.V.

"I'm gonna watch the news, we'll do homework after supper or we'll play after awhile."

I always wondered why he always watched that stupid news all the time? I mean, it's a beautiful day outside, the birds are singing, the trees and the grass is green. My brother and sister weren't there to interrupt anything! Let's just watch the news, he says!

So of course I'd get mad again and go do something else by myself.

Growing up you tend to change—and I do mean you change—a lot. Things start getting more serious as the days and years go on. You don't play as much, you

The Working Man Fights for Right

don't seem to have any interest in toys anymore, and you slowly enter the world of life.

My dad was a quiet man. He didn't have a big business or a million dollars. The one thing he did have was a love for his family and a love for his country. He also had a good job as an auto mechanic.

He fought in Vietnam and his daddy fought in World War II. Thank you for our Freedom. The news sometimes—but not all the time—helped my dad keep his family safe and let him know what was going on in the world.

As I grew older I slowly changed and also started watching the news after work most of the time. My kids get mad at me now, and so it goes. But there is a reason why we change.

We grow up to take on more responsibilities; emotionally, spiritually, physically and financially. I also want to point out my wife and children. They have inspired me to share my feelings and opinions with you. The moment you start a new job, your life changes. The moment you start a family your life changes. When you buy a new car, or a house you're in it for the long term. When you find Christ, you are saved. (I will touch on that later.)

When you grow up and get older things change around you. They change so much and you don't even

❧

realize it. This is why my dad watched the news all the time, because you know what? People need to wash their eyes out and wake the hell up. To clean out their ears and start using them.

We have had great presidents and some bad ones, too. President Reagan was a pretty damn good one I think. The Bushes were okay. I liked the son better. Now Clinton, he was playing with fire. And I don't mean a flame. There were some hot things going on under that desk and unbelievably the desk never burned.

Now some of the other presidents, well I was just too young to care. Keep in mind that every president has his negative points. The issue I have with these tough times we have now is I believe my Freedom and my children's Freedom is on the line.

I am older now and I am fully aware of my surroundings for my family and for myself. The economy always has a high side in which everything is doing well. Then there is the low side when values decrease. The president we have now is only worried about his own power. And I will point out my reasons for believing this throughout the book.

I am the ordinary working man speaking to America through each chapter and my hope is that the people shall never sleep with both eyes closed again.

The Working Man Fights for Right

And hopefully the ideas related in this book will change your life for the better.

CHAPTER 1

A Texan's View on the Economy

I intend to be very up front in this book and I am going to speak the truth. Americans are lacking the truth these days so this is the way I see it. I want Americans to get the picture in their heads about our government and the administration we have now. I'm from Texas and proud of it. A lot of people think we are just a bunch of rednecks down here, and that's okay, because Texas is going to be carrying the country's load through this whole economic downturn.

The Working Man Fights for Right

໑

We work hard for our money. Some people work with a white collar shirt and tie. We like to work with a T-shirt and steel toed boots on. Maybe even wear a cowboy hat and carry a bull whip in the toolbox of our one ton trucks. We know what a working man stands for and it isn't big government and higher taxes.

We know work and this book will tell you all about it— from the working man to the entrepreneur across this great land called America. So saddle up and get ready for my thoughts on our lives today and for tomorrow.

We live in the land of opportunity and the rest of the world knows it, but sadly our government doesn't see it that way. This is how We The People of America see it. Most people won't agree with what I am writing here but by the time I'm finished with this chapter, some will. I am a conservative and have a true belief in God and what is right for my family, my state, America, and myself.

The economy isn't the best subject to think about, but really it's everything most people do think about. What is happening to the U.S.A. is not good. This country was built from the minds, sweat, and physical and mental endurance of the working man. This is what makes this country, people working towards a goal in life. Nowadays some don't have a clue what determination and desire to prosper in America is really like. They do not care, either.

What I'm seeing is dependency, laziness, and letting another power come in and tell us what to do—whether you

♉

like it or not. Some people say that's okay, but not everyone.

When someone sacrifices time away from their wife and kids to have a little more in life—because I think they do deserve the best in life—these individuals are criticized for that. Am I right? Yes.

When people see achievers and doers, they become the targets and enemies of our government, which I think is a bunch of bull. That just makes me want to build my business even more. There are a lot of people who earn their keep and some who do not do a thing. I am a small business owner and work long hours to stay above water, just like many other great Americans. I disagree with the way things are going and happening the way they are.

I believe big businesses that got carried away financially should have failed on their own. I don't want families to go under, but this is America and there are other options and avenues to take if necessary. I work hard for what I have and if I mismanage my business, that's my problem. I might not change things, but I can sure try.

America was built on entrepreneurs and risks takers. People who take risks are the ones that create jobs. People who stuck their necks out for others and their families are now being punished. This is not the American way. The government created this mess and they are not going to be the ones to fix it. Government is the problem. We the People cannot let this happen. There are too many handouts and not enough leadership. The motivation, determination, and the desire to be somebody is sadly decreasing. The fantasy land better known as Washington, D.C., wants American's to seek dependency, and they are well on their way to seeing our country go down the drain. In other words, more inflation is on its way. More businesses will go under and more jobs will be lost. People will have to change their ways, even if I have to ride my jackass to work instead of my three-quarter-ton gas guzzler. I need to fix my problems, not bring everyone down with me. I hope things turn around for the better. Our only hope is to turn to God. I will keep pushing forward until I can't push anymore. Stay positive America.

It does not matter if you are red, white, purple, black, or violet blue. My favorite color is blue. So do you think the other colors I mentioned will call me a racist for only liking the color blue the most? The way things are nowadays, I wouldn't doubt it. The people of our country need to be taken care of but the policies are crippling our country, and that to me is scary.

We are living in fast forward with our government. What kind of leader can lead a country when his own team doesn't know what exactly it is that he wants to do? I think that is just plain chaos. The people are the ones getting punished for his success; President Obama's success. He doesn't care that he is trying to be on top and hurts people to get there.

When you want to be successful you do not hurt people on your way to the top. This president has a chip on his

❧

shoulder and it is not a potato chip. I don't think he likes America. If he wants to be like all of the other countries, he should have run for president overseas. The people of this great country know what it takes to stay strong and continue to build this country up. So when you get lied to during the campaign you have been had.

Some Presidents or politicians are really in the business for their own success. When are we ever going to hear the truth about our policies and laws so that we can still have a good life? The people want the truth about things, not just another program here or a program there. Stop holding your hand out for your success.

Mr. President, the people don't care about your dog or your calm attitude. We just want a president, not a movie star. The people just want some good living standards while not killing other things at the same time.

Whenever there is an election who gets hurt when things go bad? The People do.

When a bill gets forced down your esophagus, who gets the shaft at the end of the day? You do, the People. After all of the campaigning and all of the cheering and money being spent for one person and then that person is on his or her high horse with your dollar, what happens when bad decisions happen? Who gets hurt? We the People do. Now with all of that being said. It all boils down to what the people want.

Once our leaders are in there, they seem to think they are finished when really their work for us has just begun. I mean,

୬

that's why we voted for them, right? Our country survives on the People, not the leader. Well... Maybe, maybe not. At the day's end, if jobs aren't there or if there is not any money in the bank for a business to keep going, well, we are just out of luck, aren't we?

Why can't we have some loyalty from our leaders? Have the people lost their touch or have our leaders caught on to us? Is this happening to the people now? Our leaders know that when they run for office they will tell you what you want to hear, not what you *need* to hear. So do the people really matter to our leaders? Yes we do.

The people can make you or break you. In this case the people have been misled once again by our politicians in Washington. The lies and corruption are consuming our nation at a rapid pace and the people are frustrated and have had enough. Yes, enough is enough!

I am with you America. Tell a friend, speak out, and do it again. Do it until we get our America back. Do you know why? Because this country matters to the People and The People matter to the country.

The Working Man and The Entrepreneur: These are fighting words to our Government. If you have not felt any anger yet, you will now.

First of all, this is my country. Put yourself in my shoes and let's say you work like me and feel like me. I know you don't know me. You might say, "Damn! This guy is an ass," or you might say: *I'm glad I read this, because now I'm more educated, more informed about what is going on!* and then realize that *I knew I loved my family and country—and most of all God, but now it is all clear to me that I will fight for freedom, even if it kills me! I will be the person who I want to be and no one will ever change that!*

I feel it's time we get positive about ourselves and our accomplishments in life. We are the backbone of this country; the working man, the small business owner, and the entrepreneur.

These types of people make this country work. The working man doesn't sit on his behind for anything. A working man works from dawn to dusk, and dusk until dawn.

He can skin a buck and run a trout line—and a country boy can survive. A working man knows progress, he knows direction, and he knows how to take care of his most important objective in his life: his own family.

We focus on daily goals and long term goals. A person like this does whatever it takes to put food on the table and a roof over his family's heads—and clothes on their bodies. He also minds his own business and does things the right way.

The entrepreneur adheres to these same guidelines and motivations for his or her success. That's right ladies, I haven't forgotten about you. You women are to be thanked for America's success as equally as the men.

The Working Man Fights for Right

✤

Anyways people like you and me sacrifice a lot. We stay very busy and stressed out a lot of times in our lives. We are the people who have a good work ethic and have a passion for prosperity. You have to be around positive people as much as possible. We have a lot of negative things going on around us now, so we have to stay focused on our goals and the directions we want to go in life, with little time for distractions.

A positive person never gives up on anything. If they fail at something they try something else. If you do happen to have some money in the bank, I don't know about you, but I want a little more in there. There is always room for improvement; the sky's the limit on your success. You have to keep pushing forward to become successful. Don't ever stop just because something didn't go right the first time, or you failed. There is no failure, it is just part of life, and you have to train yourself to understand that.

We like to take chances and stretch our necks out more than others and that's the difference to being more successful or not. Doesn't it feel good to do something extra on the side to make more money and be a more powerful provider for your family or business?

One job is fine, but when you can really push forward and see achievement in your life and others', that's nothing short of awesome!!

You see, the working man and the entrepreneur creates jobs and improves communities without taking from everyone in the process. Oh, that's the government's job! We *build* businesses and improve areas for people. Whereas the government programs make all the working people dish out for people who aren't lifting a finger for anything. And Obama calls that spreading the wealth. I call it higher taxes and screwing achievers that make this country grow.

My friend, we are headed into unknown territory. We have to stay focused on keeping our businesses and jobs running the right way and in a good way to stay profitable. I *am* sorry, did I say the word profitable? The government does not like individuals who make profits. And at the same time, the government profits from all of the people and fills their pockets with no problem.

But the achievers are the backbone of this great country. We have a passion for wanting a little more in life and also to provide for others in an orderly and common sense manner.

Let's take the farmer, for example.

He has land and he breaks the land with his plow. He works long hours to plant the seeds for the future harvest in the summer and into the fall. The American Farmer provides food for people all over the world. Farming is a hard life. A lot of repetition and penny pinching. You have to really watch the fuel and fertilizer costs throughout the year. The weather is also a gamble. Is it ever going to rain again? Or when is it going to *stop* raining?

Our farmers keep us alive. The farmer works long hours in the fields. They go back and forth all day long, up and

∽

down the field. You would think that would get tiring but they do it anyway. When your family depends on a successful harvest, that is what you do.

During harvest, the farmer runs the combines and auger buggies from late morning and—if the weather is right—all the way until dark. The government doesn't realize that if they want to choke the farmers of America they, too, will go hungry. Without the farmer no one eats—even the government. That goes for both here and abroad.

Makes you wonder why things are getting so hard for the farmer to make a living when they are who produce foods for everyone. People don't realize how much work our farmers do for us day in and day out. Endless hours, and endless break downs throughout the year, but they keep ginning away at the life that they love.

Generation after generation, the land keeps getting plowed and they just take the tractor out for another round for you and me, right here in America. God bless our farmers, and keep giving them the strength to provide for us.

This might be a good time to point out a few working people and entrepreneurs. I would like to thank them for their hard work and their endless desire to be better.

Let's take the truck driver.

A truck driver leaves early in the morning and may not come back home for a couple of days, or maybe even a weeks. These guys and gals get the produce to and from grocery stores for everyone. They also could be hauling feed to and

_ℛ_

from feed mills or ports along the coast line. A trucker makes good money as long as fuel costs aren't exploding through the roof.

You see, the truck driver is the reason the stores can open for business. He brings in the goods, and then the employees come on out and get him unloaded. The store people stock the store with the goods and in return sell the products they stock at a profit.

Have you ever heard someone bitch about a truck driver? And at the same time their belly is full at suppertime, after that driver delivered to that person's store. The truck driver has a somewhat lonely life depending on how you look at it.

You can see drivers all over and look at their license plates and you can see where they pretty much are from. It's amazing how far one man or woman will drive to deliver that load. A trucker knows what it means to work for a living.

When you are gone for weeks at a time you have a responsibility to keep that tractor trailer rolling down the road and make your boss man money and some for yourself, too. That is a big machine rumbling down the highways and it is not easy to maneuver sometimes. It seems like every time you turn around there is a scale house you are forced to pull into while driving down the Interstates.

For those of you in Washington who do not know what a scale house is, please read on. It is a place where tractor-trailers pull in to weigh their loads. We have to deal with a lot out there and we really do earn our money even though we sit

ളം

on our butts ten or twelve hours a day. Rain, sleet, or snow, we know where to go. Up early and late to bed in our little sleepers. Trucking is what we love and delivering the goods is what we do. So don't slow us down out there.

The Small Business Owner plays a major role in America's economy.

The profitable small business man is the government target now, since Mr. Obama came into the White House. These people provide an economy for everyone. We do not sit around all day and twiddle our thumbs We are steadily trying to uplift our employees to do a good job. We lose a lot of time away from our families, but, like I always say, "Get up! Let's get to work..."

Who is one of the first persons to arrive at a business before the sun comes up? The small business owner. We have a lot on our shoulders because we pretty well run the show all day and some nights, too.

We have a small core of employees, but it is worth every minute. We have a closeness with our workers because we aren't in some high rise far away from our work. We are on top of every penny that goes into the business and that goes out. We are living the American Dream and taking risks for our families and our future. We truly are the backbone of this great country. Why doesn't the government see this?

I just wanted to point out that I have my hands full like a lot of others do. My cell phone never stops ringing. My repairs

ح

never stop at my rental properties, and my cattle and deer never stop eating. And still I drive full-time and have a family. How do we do it? We ask ourselves some days, is it worth it? Is it worth all the worry, all the cuts and tears that appear in your clothing while working hard? And all the calluses on your hands over the years of providing a better life for you, your wife, and most of all, your kids? You're damn right it is worth it! This is America. This is where you can freely have a life of your own and build it as big as you want, be all you can be and be good at it.

I have a duty here on earth and it is to use the strength and the muscles that God has given me to be a Free American. The auto mechanic should also be recognized. These people have a really dirty job, but they love every minute of it. My dad was an mechanic and he had the blisters, cuts, and skinned knuckles to prove it. Being a mechanic was his passion.

A mechanic loves the oil and grease that keeps a vehicle running smoothly. God bless the GM companies that got shut down for no reason whatsoever across this great land. Thank you, President Obama. The auto worker is one of those who you can never forget. That is a dirty job, but someone has to do it. This control over the dealers is not our America. Small dealerships getting letters in small towns across the nation is depressing as it gets. To be shut down, while minding their own business is pretty sad. Everybody is wondering what will be next? Just leave it up to Washington, I'm sure they will

ᦞ

think of something. And it will not be for the auto mechanic either.

We can't forget about our waitresses and waiters, doctors and nurses. These hard working people are on their feet all day long, twelve to fifteen hours a day depending on how busy the day is; maybe they are on their feet even longer.

Let's not take away from the people who provide so much for their fellow Americans. Leave our health care plans alone and put away unnecessary regulations. Let people cook what they want to cook. And let people eat what they want to eat. After all our leaders do what they want to do.

Teachers, Teachers, Teachers... Some get little pay, others a little more. This is a special person and a loving person to enhance their students knowledge levels. When you handle a bunch of kids all day, I have to tip my hat to every one of you out there. These are people who develop and sculpt children into sharp, well-mannered adults.

We cannot forget the janitors and cleaning people big companies hire. These people keep the workplace clean and sanitary for everyone who comes in the next day to work. The big boss man's job is a lot easier because of these great individuals; the good people out there who clean your toilet seats and sweep your floors in your big high rises in the big cities and small towns. People have forgotten the true working people in this land. If it wasn't for strong individuals like this our big wigs would not be the people they make themselves out to be.

ॐ

The plumbers across the land and the carpenters, and also the electricians are all reliable people who keep businesses afloat. Americans are hard working people, but these guys make everyone else's life a whole lot easier. People need to remember that the next time a problem occurs and you gripe about it, and you quickly find out you need these people more than you know.

The stay-at-home mom. Now here is a job. The women at home have more than an agenda to conquer every single day. While some men go to work, the mom starts her day with the kids, school, groceries, dishes, clothes, and PTA meetings. Guys, where is the help here? The stay-at-home moms can hold their own. After a hundred errands, then it is off to soccer, cheer leading practice, or aerobics. Then maybe a bill here and there. Supper and baths, a short kiss for the husband and a glass of wine, then off to bed. That made me tired just writing about it. God bless the stay-at-home mom.

Men, I would encourage you to show a little more respect to your wives in areas where needed, because they have a real tough job: that is, taking care of YOU. Without our spouses we would not be able to be a working man.

One occupation I haven't brought to your attention is one of the most dangerous ones. The convenience store clerk. The late night worker has to deal with all of the night owls that come out. These people have a serious job, believe it or not. When the sun goes down some odd people come out of the woodwork and visit the nearby Quick Stop. You never know what can happen because most of the time the store clerk is the only one in the store.

Each of these people makes our country what it is today. These services make the U.S.A. the best place to be on earth.

This creates an economy and avenues for people to be who they want to be and go as far as they choose to go in life. The working people are passionate and good at what they do. Also, our entrepreneurs keep things going too.

If our government keeps doing what they are doing this will decrease our value of businesses and individual freedoms to build things on our own, and people aren't going to work hard anymore.

When government comes into our lives too heavy and thick, our lives are not our lives anymore, and that isn't the American way. So keep an eye on big government, because it's here and it is building fast. Your taxes are going up as you read this and your businesses are under assault on private sector freedoms. Don't let this happen America, I have faith in you.

We have to keep accomplishing our goals and keep going in a direction that is going upwards. The direction for the workingman, that is. After all, we are entrepreneurs because we love CAPITALISM—more time to have fun and more money in my pocket for another day. I don't want to just talk about money but life without it, well, uh, kinda sucks don't it?

❧

Excuse me I didn't have my teleprompter in front of me, that's where the "uh" came from.

The word capitalism is a bad word, so they say, but who cares! We love it! The people who love that word are the same people who keep this country a float. Keep it up America, we will succeed in troubled times, we just can't forget our roots. We know what is right, and right now the big G is spending and hyper inflation will be bad.

Big Government is forgetting who built this country. The working man built up Washington, D.C. The working man built the foundation of this great nation. Working people know how it feels to work for something and earn it. Think about this: If you give a rich man a million dollars, chances are that in one year he will be even richer or still have the million dollars. If you give a poor person a million dollars, well, that person will more than likely blow through it and fundamentally be even poorer. I like to try to talk like Obama. Fundamentally is one of his favorite words.

My father-in-law told me one day, "Son, you have to build a business slowly. If you jump too fast or miss certain things along the way, it could be very costly."

I thought to myself, kind of like eating too fast. The food looks delicious but if you swallow without chewing first chances are you will throw it up. That chicken fried steak and German potatoes and an apple pie on the side for dessert won't look too good all thrown up on the ground will it?

The Working Man Fights for Right

୭

That sounds like our administration, don't it? Shoving programs down our throats so fast that our own leaders don't even know what the hell is going on. And we are supposed to trust them?

I want to also recognize the firefighter, and the police man. Without the courage and strength of the minds and hearts of these men and women we would not have the safe and secure lives that we enjoy. Our investments, our homes, and our loved ones remain protected for another day. Remember we have our own mind to use in these troubled times. We do not and will not flock towards dependency from some other source. We are Americans so let's start acting like Americans.

Working man, I can relate to you and you are not alone. America, we will not fail. After all, we know what it takes after we hit bottom. We just dust ourselves off and get back up and start all over again.

CHAPTER 2

Our Kids are Our Future

Take a look at your kids and pray. When I watch the television news I think of my kids. I am getting older and wondering what Texas and the USA will be like in two years, or ten years, or even twenty-five years? There is just nothing coming out of Washington, D.C. that is really working for the working people. I believe what Obama wants is to suck the blood out of the private sector. Government jobs really keep this country going. It seems our leader wants to lead a poor country.

The Working Man Fights for Right

America is not a poor country by definition, but it seems more and more to me that that is what he wants. Does he want us to be his little peasants and follow him around like little ducklings do with their mommy?

I pray for my kids and hope this doesn't destroy their lives like he is destroying ours as grownups. You cannot have one man in charge of all of your business and personal privacy and expect to enjoy a prosperous life.

Our president thinks he is a savior, but he is sadly mistaken. My family and I have one Savior and he is Jesus Christ. I try to teach my kids a real and true way to live, work, and earn their keep. Notice I didn't say fair share. My kids aren't taught to hold their hands out. Taking from one to give to another who didn't do a damn thing for it is totally wrong. This is who are President is.

The President would be living in a slum if it wasn't for our Founding Fathers who laid the foundation for all of us; who love the freedom that is. What I'm getting at here is when you close down businesses for no reason, fire people for no reason—especially when the president has no damn business sticking his nose in private businesses anyway—it is nothing more than a massive power grab to choke this nation.

My kids have two parents: my wife and me. Parents remember this... No one will ever teach or discipline your kids better than you can. This government daycare bull-puckey where they think they have all the answers is a bunch of crap. Government needs to back off and leave our kids alone and leave us alone to take care of them. That is why *I'm* the parent, not the Washington wannabe decision makers. My kids will not be corrupted by this government, ever. I'll see to that.

Okay, I'll simmer down a little bit. I sit in my living room and see my baby daughter lying there on the living room floor. She has her pillow and blankie and always likes for me to lay down with her on the floor. But sometimes it is more fun to just watch her lay there and think of her future. It is a special moment in time.

When I see my little girl with the world the way it is I just can't help but think of the way her life could possibly be if we continue to be consumed by a government that doesn't care about protecting true freedom. Do parents really want some administration—whatever political side it may be on—to control your kids like they are attempting to control us right now? And if we don't stop this, what is the outcome?

Let's think about how we can be better parents in every way possible because our kids need us now more than ever There are some nights when my baby girl falls asleep on the living room floor. I could have simply put her in bed but these moments won't be around forever. I said a prayer to God as I watched her sleep, her little hand holding mine.

"Lord, protect my little girl. Guide her, sculpt her into a strong, independent individual as she grows up in an ever changing world. Help her realize that she has to stay prepared and focused on her surroundings. Daddy won't be around all the time, but when you call me up, I'll watch over her from the heavens, Amen."

I can remember the day our baby girl was born. Tears of joy ran down my wife's face and mine. I told her I loved her and we kissed. The moment we held our daughter in our arms was a blessing from God. I looked into my baby girl's eyes and at that moment I can truthfully say I saw God.

You parents have to teach your kids reality. We cannot allow our kids to grow up in a nation that will not let them fail. They need to experience struggles and bumps in the road. Their lives cannot be lived through a governmental hand, never being allowed to hit the ground while trying to be their own person. This totally defeats the purpose of God putting us on earth. This will not make a child stronger.

Let me explain. Take a body builder that lifts weights every day. How did he or she get to be that muscular? After a reasonable amount of time the body builder put more and more weight on the bar so it got harder and harder every day to every month that they lifted. Okay, so instead of being non-muscular and just being mediocre, the person who put some resistance and a little pain on their body is healthier and in a lot better shape.

Putting a few obstacles in life, like a little pain and a few struggles, will give your life more meaning than just saying, "Oh well, I don't need to do all of that work... I'll be fine."

It seems that no one wants to work anymore under this type of government. Parents of America remember this, never forget how your kids got to where they are today or where they will be in the future. They got there by your guidance and knowledge, and blessings from God. No government can ever accomplish what you have. I am not going to tell you what to do with your kids, but what I am going to do is encourage you to never take them for granted.

Our kids will only be babies for so long. Even though my daughter will always be my little girl, eventually she will become her own person and tell me she is an adult and can take care of herself. Those are the words that you dread hearing while you are a parent.

Our children need our guidance more now than ever. And misleading our children in our current society is sometimes scary when our kids appear sometimes to know more than we do. Sometimes what they know is not what they need to know to push forward with their lives in the right way. Our kids need to be kids.

Give them that time to grow and to enjoy their young lives. Always talk to them and encourage them. Let them know that they can be winners in life. Let them know that sometimes they will experience failure and sometimes success. Most of the time to be very successful you will experience some failures. Just remember to tell your young ones that this is part of life. We will never know how far we can go unless we go that extra mile and try to reach our full potential.

We can only give our kids so much advice that is really going to sink in. We get so worried when they go out on a

The Working Man Fights for Right

❧

Friday night. We give them the speech about being an angel, thinking in the back of our own heads, *God, I hope they don't do what I used to do.* When they come home thirty minutes late we are all upset, knowing at the same time that we did the exact same thing when we were young. How can we get mad at them?

These are all learning experiences between a kid and a parent or parents. No one can really tell you how to raise your kids. That is all done in the privacy of your own home. So how can government think they know all of the answers for our own kids? In reality they really don't. They are just fooling themselves hoping you will depend on them for that, too.

Being a parent is a full-time job. Pretty much 24/7, until the day we die. Even when they move out, our kids are on our minds every minute of the day. Then when you become a grandpa or grandma, your grandbabies join the worry wagon and the process starts all over again.

Please stay focused on the direction your children's lives are headed. No one else will. We still have full control over our lives and our kids. No government of any kind will ever take that away from us. We have the final decision, the last word, and the right to speak up for us and our children.

When I say look at your kids and pray, what goes through your mind? What does the Working Man mean? I mean that I know what it is like in the real world, and the real world has no mercy on someone's life. Life is

❧

tough. Days go by so fast that you just don't know where the time went. One day you blink your eyes and realize that you went from being eighteen years old to thirty in a heartbeat. As you get older life pretty much flies by. We have to have a plan for our lives and I don't mean a government program that will tax our kids even more than they are now.

I mean that you must develop a direction for your kids that include prosperous goals and abundant lives. Your kids may think they know everything, but the parent is still there to help along the way. Like I said earlier, we can only do so much. Our children will have to learn from their own mistakes and grow from that. In other words, it is called Life.

Even though our kids are hard headed sometimes we have to learn to let it go in a special way. We were hard headed when we were young (and some of us still are). Not to malign the purpose of being a parent, we need to remember how we were back then. The best bet is to be a role model for your children. Be someone who loves life. Be someone who helps others and doesn't expect anything in return. And remember that you will do anything for your children, even if it means taking a bullet for them or giving them your last breath. You will always find a way to help and protect your kids.

Teach them the freedom we have in America; freedom to be whoever we want to be. Teach them that this is the land of opportunity. Show them what it means to earn a dollar and not just wait for one to drop into their pocket from Uncle Sam.

The Working Man Fights for Right

Giving people money makes them weak and we certainly have a lot of that going on now.

Explain to them that their dreams can come true. They will become who they want to be. No one should ever have the right to take that away from them in this great country we call America. And no one will ever come between the parent and our children. Not even the biggest government like the one we are faced with now.

This is why I look at my kids and pray.

CHAPTER 3

Remember Freedom?

D o you remember when people just went to work and minded their own business? People worked hard and focused on putting food on the table from day to day. We felt secure, calm, and enjoyed our lives. My grandparents always said those were the good old days. We did have issues back then but we got through them. It wasn't this or that, you just did what you were supposed to do and that was that.

What we do today is screw people, lie to people, and take

∽

them for a ride without them knowing they have even been on a ride.

America is becoming a cutthroat nation; through our politicians and the organizations behind the scenes and the ones that fly under the radar. America, our freedoms are disappearing and are fading fast. People need to realize that our country is fast becoming another nation.

This administration is poking its nose into everyone's business, and at the same time they think they will save the planet. Why change a nation of freedom? I'm so tired of the word *change* I don't even want to change my underwear anymore. The government wants to force you into a little car, and force you to not smoke anymore (even though they can). They take over companies for no reason and they act like it's nothing but a thing. The policies that are being pushed through have nothing to do about freedom in this country.

Washington's objective is to destroy the private sector from the west coast to the east. That's some change we can believe in. Our president now wants to fundamentally transform this country. He said this five days before he became president in 2009 and he is now exercising one of the objectives on his list.

He does not have a plan for the people of this country, he has a plan for his civilian group to become the military in government at home; to control this country his way. Our president won't consider drilling here in the USA, but it's okay to talk with Brazil and help them out on oil situations.

⦿

Michele Obama is finally proud to be an American, since her husband is now the president. I wonder about that. I have been proud to be an American since I've been wet behind the ears. My friend, what the hell is wrong with this country?! It's amazing how a salesman can come in here and become president and roll over everyone in his path.

The working man has built this country. The poor will get poorer and the middle class will soon join them because of these programs that are designed to build Big Government. They are in the process of destroying and corrupting the work ethic that this country once had. It will be a cold day in hell when I hold my hand out to this government.

Remember when we could go out and buy whatever we wanted and no one cared. Now there are so many nosy programs interfering with what we want to buy. Food, clothes, water, jets, large trucks, fuel, need I go on? If you want to eat a hamburger then do it. If you want to eat a pizza with six different toppings, then do it. Let me put it this way, if it is okay for our leaders to live like kings then what is the problem in letting the people live like them too? Oh, must be a control thing. I'm telling you out there, wherever you are, that our freedoms are slowly disappearing before our eyes. Maybe this will wake you up. I think you know how I feel about my beautiful country by now. Enough is enough already .

The Working Man Fights for Right

୨ଡ଼

Here are some more destruction of Freedom issues. We are moving towards fascism in this country. Our politicians are running too much already. The Private Sector isn't the Private Sector anymore. Bill Aires has also worked under the radar. There are organizations working against us and it is not good.

The stimulus and all the bailouts of the banks, General Motors, insurance companies are to me just techniques and strategies to build Bigger Government, because government thinks you can't experience any pain or struggles in your life or failure. Those three things right there are the keys to your success in life. If this isn't a takeover of our Freedoms I don't know what is. America , there is a warm wind coming in off of the ocean and it's no breeze, it's a freakin' storm. And it is going to be more than a hurricane.

Protect yourself, protect your kids, and protect your investments. One more thing: keep God first in your life. He is our only answer. I repeat, *our only answer.*

Have you noticed all of the working people around you? We wake up early in the mornings (or maybe some work nights) and we hit the ground running. We drive to work and start our busy day. I look out across the city streets, the ship channel at the Port of Houston and also across the fields along the Texas highways. You talk about turning the wheels to start up our economy every morning, look around you. People take time away from their families to provide a

◈

better life for them. This is the Freedom we have in this great country. The American worker greases the wheels to push businesses to the highest level of production every day.

The blood that flows through the veins of the American people make this nation what it is. If we don't have jobs we do not have a prosperous nation. The stimulus package did not do anything. We have to keep the jobs going here in America, not pick and choose who you like and dislike. People put in long hours to make ends meet and it is not easy but that is what makes a wealthy nation.

When is government going to see that increasing everything around us is not going to work? With all of the changes happening so fast and having a leadership that doesn't know what is going on down here on earth, we really have to protect ourselves financially and make the right choices. At least the ones we have left, am I right?

Our children will become so gun shy that they might think it's not worth it to work. The cost of living is too high, depending on where you live. The fuel will be too high for our cars and trucks . The energy costs will be higher also. So if you want to see abundance, all of these items that we need to live with will have to come down.

Business owners are struggling and worried about their investments and how many people they will be able to keep on their work force. Every program that the government talks about or tries to push through is just another paycheck for

The Working Man Fights for Right

Washington and less for the people who make this country operate.

We have to keep the Private Sector private and free from any more regulation. I understand we have rules and regulations, but when you abuse them and use them to destroy profitable business, that is wrong.

We are trying to pinch our pennies and make it through this tough financial time. If the policies keep being pushed through we will not have the America we have today for our children tomorrow. This is an assault on our country from the inside out. Who in the hell did we vote for?

Why spread the wealth when you should be teaching that person skills to be better and more knowledgeable. Why take from faithful working people and entrepreneurs who have lived the American dream and give it to somebody who has the exact same brain, two hands, two feet, two legs, a mouth and ears, and a nose, who doesn't care about the good things in life?

Let me put it to you straight. If little Johnny wants to sit there and suck on his hind tit, well I guess it's time he gets winged and put out to the pasture and become a bull of his own kind and experience the life that God gave him.

People who understand life and can comprehend it understand that a comfortable life or an abundant life is the best way to go. That's why you see all of these cars and trucks on the highways, because those people are going after their dreams.

❧

Yes, we may pay higher taxes, but they are not giving up on themselves or family. But when you have the guiding light of government to shine down upon you, too many people, I said *too many damn people*, think it is okay! Once you encourage that mentality, America is finished. You might as well call us France.

I am confident that this will not happen. But we have to stop the change and put our dollars back in our pockets, not the government's. Do some deals. Open up a new business. Get people more to building and keeping this economy in an upward motion. Stretch your neck out and help me save this country. We need each other more than ever. And after a hard day's work we pick up our kids and we see our wives, husbands, (or whatever kind of date we have) and we enjoy life.

We help with homework or cook supper together, or maybe even continue to do a side job to provide for our families. And guess what, tomorrow there may be double the traffic on the roads, and do you know why? The people that make this country great got off of their butts and said, "I can do this. I can take care of myself. I'll be a great employee, I will be a prosperous business owner or someone who wants to stay free in America and live to the fullest and work hard for this country that we all love so dearly."

Don't sit down yet! There is work to be done.

CHAPTER 4

The Politicians Should Live Like Us

Our politicians need to experience the way a real American lives. What if our leaders had all of these Washington regulations hanging over their heads? Would they be so enthused about them then? Would they be happy about where their lives are going ? Ask yourself, don't these questions just piss you off? You already know what the answer is for me. From the first page of this book, you know my feelings. So to the great leaders of our country, tell me, why aren't your lives affected by these forced programs and artificial rules and regulations? You could not live even one day under these stresses and forced regulatory spider webs. So why punish the people who voted you in? You were supposed to lead us to better lives and improve our communities through better government. But as far as I can tell, you've just done the opposite.

We should not have to tolerate these kinds of actions upon our citizens across the land. After all, the people built this country but we just happen to get the short end of the stick. At least this time around. Right now is the time to make a difference in America while we all have the choices and freedom to do what we need to do.

Why not tell the president what to eat? Why don't we tell him to quit smoking? Why don't we paint him into an economic a corner with no other options and say, "This will pass no matter what, because Prince Harry Reid said so." Put the shoe on the other foot and sit down and imagine it. The American people aren't stupid.

You government folk may not have liked the way America operated in the past, but you are not going to waltz into our private lives and take away everything and anything you want. It does not work that way. I know for a fact that I have never experienced losses and stresses like I feel now. And the bad part of it is that I'm losing control of everything I hold dear and the government knows it and keeps on eating, and eating, and eating at the Working Man anyway.

The Working Man Fights for Right

≈

No one will tell me not to eat or drink. No one will tell me what truck to buy or how much fuel to use. I make those decisions.

What happened to our choices? This is The United States of America. This is not the America that I want my kids to grow up in. Can someone hear me? These need to stop trying to tell my wife, kids and me how to live. And I mean this needs to stop right now!

Our leaders need to start feeling the peoples' pain, and I am certain that if they did, they would never tolerate this at all. So why are the leaders treating us like this? The simple answer is that they love control and can't get enough of it. But it will be a cold day in hell when the government thinks they will tell my family what to do with our own lives and businesses. This is utter bull.

We are the dreamers, doers, and achievers who make this country work. This mess will only get worse if they think we are going to live like this. This nation did not get this far by sitting on our butts and the people will not tolerate this behavior any longer.

And I would ask the politicians, *Who wants to lead a poor country?* Personally, I'd like to be a leader of a strong, enthusiastic, thriving, and smart country, wouldn't you? Just because President Obama was poor and happened to get the breaks, like he said, doesn't mean that we all have to be forced into being poor!

❧

L et's ask the government a few questions.

- Do you want higher taxes?

- Do you want someone telling your kids what to do or how to live?

- Would you like someone to take your hard earned money and give it to somebody else who did not do a damn thing to earn it?

- Do you want Death Care to be forced down your throat and be called un-American because you had a question about it?

- Do you want the people to sell you on some high dollar program that we know we cannot afford to do, and then lie about it the rest of your term?

These are all good questions aren't they? You know, it is always easier to sign this and sign that sitting while behind a desk. It's always easier to force unwitting people into programs that they didn't even want instead of talking to them face to face.

Our leadership needs to feel and live like the average American does. They need to get some trust back and some ço

reality in their heads. They need to really see what's going on with the original, true American person. I know they are our leaders. I just want our government to display a little respect and common sense now and then. After all, we got them there. And you know the beautiful thing about all of this? This is America and we can kick them out just as easily, and don't let my dollar bill hit you where the Good Lord split you on your way out the door.

The bottom line is that this is the greatest country on earth. This is America and we have freedom for a reason. People have the liberty to do what they want to do and the president and his administration are not God. They might think they know it all, but they don't. Since they crave change so much, let's make the leaders change their ways.

I believe Washington has forgotten what freedom is all about. The drive to keep the people free in this country has been derailed by a bigger government with false hopes through various programs that if they pass will ultimately destroy America as we know her.

Hope and Change was only meant for the people who really need some hope and change in their lives. So stop forcing false hopes and dangerous changes down our throats . When the tables turn, in the end the people of this great nation will be the leading force. And we cannot afford to be silent anymore.

CHAPTER 5

Obama Care Equals
Death Care

I know that everybody wants go to Heaven, but few want to go now. Let's get one thing clear. I love helping people. I am one of those guys who doesn't mind giving a helping hand any time of the day or night. Now, with that being said, the problem we American's have (or let's say most American's have) is the unlimited invasion of our privacy such as openly revealing our personal medical records.

The Working Man Fights for Right

Now the government is forcing us to bend over and check us out from both ends whether we like it or not. Where did our rights go? When did our choices disappear?

As the hand of Obama comes down and caresses our cheek we will find that we are paralyzed into government servitude for all creation.

We have some serious issues right smack in front of us. Our lives are being played with. My family is my responsibility and no one else's. What kind of world would we be living in if we had to wait for certain operations that might take two weeks or six months before finally being admitted into the hospital? Sounds like a plan doesn't it? It does for our president, because here again he will have more control over your life. How will he have control over your life?

- He will have access to your health records.

- He will have control over an operation that you need, but will tell you that you are too old to have it done, so possibly your grandma or father could pass away before they got the care they needed.

- The government will then sit there and tell you what you need to eat, drink, and also have someone there ready to talk to you when you are start to see the light .

ॐ

They don't think the family is smart enough to talk and comfort their loved ones during this tough time in. In other words, our leaders think that their team has something better to offer our own family members. Talk about arrogance.

Let me get this straight. Our government, that can't even run a cash for clunkers program that is leaving all of the dealerships out to dry, is going to tell my mom, dad, or grandparents what to do before I do? Hell No! No Way!

This is what is happening and we need to fight this and not let this one get away. If you want privacy then you had better speak up.

Do you really want someone who doesn't even know you to get this involved in your personal business? I don't know about you, but I feel that our president is angry at the United States of America. If you try to ask him about the health care program he will not answer, and you may get penalized for not using the government plan.

If our president doesn't get his way he'll eliminate our freedom of choice in America. Why else would he be planting people at the town hall meetings instead of seeking out the true Americans. This government needs to wake up and listen to the people that put them in the congressional seats. They better be ready for us because the horses are saddled, fed, and watered, and we are coming. Freedom is our objective, not the invasion of the Privacy Act.

The Working Man Fights for Right

৯০

This act of our leadership will no longer be tolerated. Someone needs to ask the people: "Who actually likes this corrupt way of caring for our loved ones?"

What if this was your mom or dad? How would you like it if somebody ordered (or let's say *forced* you into believing that this is it for your grandpa or grandma? While at the same time the life could have been saved or prolonged by the decision of the one who was sick.

We are truly faced with some off the wall issues here and we cannot be sucked in by them. Once that happens our lives as Americans will be lost .

Did we vote for a president in November, or a the subject of a photo shoot or an orator from speech class 101? Looking good on a magazine cover or acting like a model is not what we had in mind when a lot of Americans voted for change.

Our elected officials from across the country need to think about how they got where they are. It took the peoples' votes to secure their seats. And now, when we voice our opinions on real life issues, these same people couldn't care less about our feelings or figure out what is truly right for the American population.

It is a crying shame to have Washington want our country to live like Great Britain or Canada and then hear about the failures of their health care programs and still force Obama Care down our throats. What is going on with our country is very sad. This administration has no mercy, no feelings, no sincerity or compassion for the people of this country.

*

The soccer moms, the stay-at-home moms and our elderly are furious about this. Real working people are just not good enough for our president. Instead of praising people for exercising their right to freedom of speech and expressing views on serious issues, our senators and the Administration find ways to shut us up.

To those of you who are not aware of what your leaders are capable of, well, here you go.

Just because you don't like something forced down your throat (and you would rather swallow before chewing) you are now called a Hate Monger, you're part of a mob, and you are Un-American. And we voted people into office? I think it is time to really make a difference. The tides are slowly changing and the true American people are coming out of the woodwork.

This president doesn't like criticism, but if you mess with the people who built this country, well, let's just say that the party has just begun. We The People shall also add that we do not need a TelePrompTer in order to speak to America. We speak from the heart and we say what we mean and mean what we say! I Love America, and I will not tolerate losing my country over a government health program that is based on controlling otherwise free individuals while taking away their freedom to choose what they want to do.

This Obama Care plan will cut jobs of doctors and nurses across the nation. People will not get the care they need when they need it. Our veterans and so many others are getting the

❧

short end of the stick here. When everyone will get government health care, everyone will suffer and will get the shaft.

What about our cancer patients? What about all of the money individuals put into cancer research? With a little common sense all of this research could be done for almost nothing. But if people can't even get an operation until six months or more, we will be dead before our surgeries. So all of that money was spent for nothing. Is this what it has come down to? Innocent American's being forced into a plan that will ultimately limit their access to good doctors and coverage?

It is almost like cutting your finger and letting it bleed, because what's the hurry ? I won't be seen until next week. I might as well wrap it up and hope for the best. And the reason why is because the best health care days are behind us.

The next thing that will happen is that our employers won't carry insurance anymore. You are damned if you do and damned if you don't with this Administration. Let your voices be heard and be firm. This is unconstitutional. This is wrongful doing. Fight the good fight for freedom and we will prevail. We are the voice of this nation.

Pushing an artificial program that no one has even read all the way through is not the way to run a country (although it is the way to run a country in the ground). We The People know that is the main objective of the whole Obama Care program.

᪗

We are not going to be forced into using something that will ultimately hurt the American family for a very long time to come.

When you see great Americans on television literally fighting for our country's rights, doesn't that say a lot? Americans that working every day to provide for their families, and then taking the time to speak out is what America is all about. We are fighters; we are the backbone of this great nation, and that backbone will not be broken. The working men and women have come too far to allow this kind of behavior to be foisted onto their own people.

Our leaders need to take lessons from the families across the land. We will fight you tooth and nail on this because this is the peoples' land, not some group's that thinks it will force or brainwash us into another scheme, just like all of the other programs that are not good for the people. This whole government is only concerned about its own power and doesn't care at all about the people. Our Leaders haven't caught on yet but it's time they do. We are Americans and we are free and that is the way it will stay!

What would you do if the government actually told your ailing loved one that it's over? This is none of their business and it never should or will be.

Socialism is here and some people don't even realize it. Whatever you do, keep God first and pray for your family. We are going to need the prayers, trust me.

The Working Man Fights for Right

When you elect a president, you would think you'd get a person who loves freedom and will help you Pursue Happiness without taking from everyone around you. Well, I was wrong. We wanted a leader to lead the best country in the world. A president should run a country, yes. But a president should not CONTROL a country. The leaders should work with the people, not make the people do things we do not want to. The people deserve respect from you, Mr. President.

We deserve honesty, faithfulness to our country's values. We will not have this, oh, what can I call it? Rape. Raping a nation of freedom.

We are in a crisis, so our leaders preach. Well, if you keep running a country into the ground like you are, I guess crisis is what you get. Let me rephrase that; it is what the American people get, not the leaders. But I'm certain that this is what our leaders want.

This country is driving down a fast road towards a guy with a chip on his shoulder, and I don't mean a potato chip. This government-run country is, and very well may be held accountable for their actions. People in America are not and will not live their lives under a president who thinks he has all the answers to life's triumphs and troubles.

This is America and I will choose my health care, I will choose my home I want to buy, and I will choose my vehicle I want to drive. I wonder... If something goes wrong with one of these decisions will Obama take full accountability for our failures? After all, he is forcing this all down our throats. He thinks Americans cannot make decisions on their own. Will there be lawsuits for this kind of behavior? Put yourself in someone's shoes who has lost their job.

Obama decides to take a company over and the company fails. What about the Obama Care that he is pushing? What if my mom dies because she was too old for the Obama Care regulations and stipulations? Will this president be responsible for his actions? You tell me. These are innocent lives he is playing with. Some in Washington have to be held accountable.

What the government is doing to the people is going to be a disaster for our children and their children. This is no longer President Bush's fault.

Do you remember the movie *Pure Country*? George Strait played Dusty the singer. Do you remember when the band became bigger and bigger as the band got more popular and earned more green in their pockets? They got big very fast and very quickly. Their show started to have too much smoke and too many bright lights and fireworks. You couldn't even hear the song or see George singing.

Without the words there is no song, and without the songs there will be no show anymore. This is what we have now.

In other words, no one knows what is going on anymore. Our leaders are too caught up in their own fame and amassing a fortune by taking from others. People aren't upset that we are helping the poor. People are upset because this ço

administration is taking from people who have earned their own money and deserve to keep it. Obama is now crippling most people into literally having to force their well-earned money into others' hands. Hands that have not done anything to enjoy the fruits of their own labor. They prefer to eat someone else's fruit.

George Strait's people who were caught up in all the money and big shows were actually destroying his own show. Well, George then had a meeting with everyone and shortly after that he put everything back together again. He told his manager that he can do this with or without him. This is how the people of this country feel.

If you have all of these ramrods in office, more than likely your country will lose control of what the true meaning of it really was. It falls back into the peoples' laps. The people are the true foundation of this great land. And that is what is being torn apart here. But the people of this country will save it. And in the end someone will be held accountable for this, and it will not be the people. This country's future relies on us.

We cannot let any of this happen. The Working Man has worked too hard to lose this now, and now we do have our eyes open and ears pricked. Our leaders need to feel the consequences for not leading a country and for controlling what we can and cannot do. If our leaders want this kind of authority then maybe they ran for office in the wrong country. You think?

Americans do not and will not allow this behavior on our own soil. Think about who you vote for next time. Don't let someone tell you what to do all of the time. We are now suffering the consequences of false hopes that were promised to the people and in return we have an invasion of our privacy and a bigger government that does not care about the little guys who put them there.

CHAPTER 6

Losing Trust

As you can tell by now, the trust is fading regarding Obama. The dealerships are hanging out to dry right now because of the Cash for Clunkers Program. The government doesn't have any money for another program. Yes, it did help some consumers get a better car but now, since the cars are getting better fuel mileage, there may be a charge on each mile you drive because there is a drop in traffic to the gas stations. I personally love my clunker and I choose to keep it. I have enough bills to pay and the government gets enough of my somewhat backfiring or is just a big joke to the American people courtesy of the government. This, believe it or not, is a money game and they are merely screwing everyone who hasn't caught on to this yet.

This is nothing less than the total destruction of our country and slowly but surely the people are moving away from the president instead off flocking to him. Now *that* is change I can believe in. I'm Scott Filip and I approve this sentence!

We are becoming a nation of warriors and stronger people. People are finally realizing that this is the People's land and not just one man's. We The People are coming together and finding out what this administration is all about.

No one knows who to trust in Washington anymore. You see, when you about every other word that comes out of your mouth is a lie, it will eventually catch up with you down the road. Or maybe even sooner. (Let's say sooner!) Too bad we didn't figure this out in November of 2008, but hey, I love a challenge and boy do we have one now.

The Democrats get mad at all of the great Americans talking about the economy and voicing how bad things are now. (And wondering where all of this money is going to come from.)

The Working Man Fights for Right

ഇ

When people tell them to stop spending they do not care. When Bush was in the White House he was trashed for this and for that. Maturely, President Bush took it like a man. He let all the mumbo jumbo just roll off of him just like water rolling off a duck's back.

President Bush stood firm and stood proud for our country. The other countries were fully aware of his refusing to take any crap from any other country, and they knew it too.

Now we have a president that does not care what you think or how you feel, even though he pretends to show concern. But it's not what you think. This administration cannot take rejection or criticism. This administration thought this was going to be a walk in the park, but you can't expect to disrespect a president from Texas and not catch any heat while you're in the hot seat. This government thinks they are God's gift to a nation .

Approval numbers are slipping and reality is finally setting in. All of the people in this government need to step aside and let the real Americans take this country back. Was that a racial statement? I'll say it again. The real people need to take this country back. We want the truth and achievement of our forefathers. The American people are waking up and you know what? They do not have their hands out looking for a free lunch.

Obama tricked people into voting for him and now those people hate his policies, and he cannot stand it. Sounds like life to me.

❧

This man is disrespecting the same people who voted for him. Are we on an emotional, financial, and social roller coaster? Yes we are, and that is what this new administration wants. I mean, one day he is our savior and the next day he calls you out if you don't like him.

The distrust of this government is causing arguments, fights, and maybe even the possibility of a civil war in the future. These people will not listen to the other side.

When two parties differ on certain subjects, nothing ever really gets solved unless you talk it out. The government wants to shut down the voices of Americans and that is very wrong and childlike. Our Freedom of Speech is at stake here too. This USA is not a place for big government. If you want big government you are living in the wrong country. We make our own decisions in our own lives, not the government.

We have free markets here, but free is not in their vocabulary unless they are redistributing your wealth to some deadbeat who refuses to work.

Just keep lying to the people and your numbers will go down like an avalanche in the state of Alaska, (where your competition lives, and you know who she is).

If you truly want to help the people—and the key word here is truly—you will find that you ultimately succeed. The distrust in this man is steadily growing. People are angry, sad, stressed, and also just plain scared. What the hell does this government not see that we see?

The Working Man Fights for Right

ဢ

Parents are calling into the radio stations and are scared for their children, like I am for mine. Life was hard enough, before November 2008. Now our government is making it even harder for us and is getting rich at the same time. The Working Man is headed for some troubled times. We have to get them out of office. Now!

Remember when I mentioned radio? Well, I listen to it most of the day. I do drive an eighteen-wheeler for a living and at the same time I sit on my butt. Yes, I am sitting on my butt, but at the same time a paycheck is being earned during the week. Some people don't want a hand out.

I try to keep my hands in my pockets because every day of my life it seems like some kind of vacuum is sucking my money out of my pockets and I cannot control it or stop it. Our privacy is slowly disappearing, our health care options are turning into *You do what I say or you will get penalized*, and our computers are even being invaded.

Some voted for a trustworthy guy but this isn't trust in what is a troubled economy. Let's have some common sense here.

When you don't like something in the policies you should compromise, but is becoming more like these policies will be forced upon you whether you like it or not. The president preaches about Freedom of Speech and how sweet it is to have. So when some Americans open their mouths and dare to voice contrary opinions they become a target. We are not the same country we were in 2007 and 2008. This country is changing and is changing fast whether you care to believe it or not. This change in America is slowly being recognized and people are finally questioning if they have a president they can still trust. You tell me if you trust him or not.

Our leaders have been good and some have been bad over the years. One thing you can trust Obama on is that he is reshaping the country and he is very truthful about that. People just thought he had something else in mind. Turns out, he does. What he has in mind is for the good of the government not our country. That's why he needs us to do our part, or like Vice President Biden said a while back, "You have to have some skin in the game."

The other day I busted my finger while I was working on my tractor, so I guess I could say I was working hard to have some money to pay my higher taxes. Does that count? I mean, I left some skin on my tractor and had less on my hand. What more do you want?

If these changes and mutual distrust regarding our Obama government doesn't scare you as an adult, just wait until your baby girl and baby boy have to live under these rules and regulations.

What happened to our freedom to choose what we ourselves want to do? Prepare your kids for the future, because it very well may not be the country you and I grew up in. What happened to our trust? I ask myself that a lot. And you know what? I am not alone, either.

The Working Man Fights for Right

୨

The Working Man and entrepreneur always have to watch their finances, and who better to watch our finances than YOU yourself? Let's talk about money.

Money is good and yes, money can be bad. If you are an ass before you make a lot of money then after you make a lot of money, you may very well turn into an ass*hole*.

My family never had a lot of money but the money they did have they never wasted. Put yourself in my shoes and think of your parents as you read this.

If you look back on how we lived back then, think about this: we never really got ahead, but we had enough. Doesn't that sound good and ring true? We had enough. Mom and Daddy always had enough and I never went to bed hungry. Our moms and dads always — um, what's the word? — WORKED! Yeah, that's it, they worked. And they worked hard and they were also good at what they did. They provided for us and kept us safe .

Some individuals would be a lot better off financially if they would only work. But some have their hand out all the time and then somehow they always produce the rich guy to blame. But people come equipped with their own brain and can make their own decisions; it is called getting off your ass and doing something with your life.

We live in the land of opportunity. So take advantage of it. If you want some extra cash, just go mow a yard. Help a family member with some paperwork. Go haul hay or drive a tractor for a farmer and give him a break. And then, when you are done, stay there and talk to that old timer you have just helped. I guarantee you will be more knowledgeable after you leave his place. Our older folks are really very smart.

Our young people think they know everything and that, right there, is the problem with a lot of things in our lives. Most young people think they have all of the answers, but they don't. Slow your life down a little and give someone else some time to inspire you. You might not think they are doing so at the time, but give it a few weeks or even a year. When something comes up in your life down the road the first thing that will pop into your head will be that old timer who talked to you that day. You gave him a chance to talk and you benefited from it later. That is a win-win situation.

Our finances are one of the most important considerations in our lives. Our parents made it look easy because they put their money into things that prospered for them. If they didn't invest, they saved it — and they were good at it. Don't always think you know everything. Look at that old timer's bank account and compare it to yours. That's a big difference, isn't it?

Nowadays there are so many things out there to buy that distract us from saving our money. We have to be disciplined to maintain staying above water and sometimes it is really hard to keep money in your savings or checking account. We have to discipline ourselves and trust the right people. But remember, no one else will protect your money like you do.

The Working Man Fights for Right

Remember that you will be the one to financially stay up or come crumbling down in the end.

What we are seeing now is that the government thinks it knows what to do with your money better than you do. Well isn't that something?

They are hoping you give into them so they can control this part of your life also. My finances are my business, not theirs. If I want to take a few dollars out of my budget to buy a big fat juicy hamburger, then I will. If I want to eat at the local a heart attack shack, then that is my individual choice. If the government is worried about me killing myself they don't need to worry anymore, because they are killing me already.

Bailouts are nothing more than a tragedy to individual businesses and the people at large. Now what you have is businesses that are failing anyway and small businesses that are struggling more than ever. Chalk another one up for the government.

Now the people who once provided for the poor are going to be even poorer in the future, but nowadays that seems to be the norm. Just tear down someone who worked for something good and was actually headed in a good direction in life. What a way to teach prosperity.

We have a lot of good people who have given their blood, sweat, and tears for their families and now our taxes will be so high in the future. So many just don't realize what is going on around them.

∽

The stimulus package is another signing party for our president. Meanwhile, the dollar is falling as the minutes go by.

On October 29, 2009 the value of the dollar fell to 63 cents. My grandparents would be furious at the actions that this administration is forcing on innocent Americans now. Our finances are being swiped away before our eyes. The 401k's are sadly decreased and most savings accounts are totally gone. The stock market is shaky, the economy is shaky, and my America is shaky.

We have an administration that says build a business, chase your dreams, and become who you want to be. Well, probably so he can control whatever you will have accomplished and achieved so they can again step in and oversee everything you do. That is the plan for this administration. They won't come out and say it, but anyone with eyeballs and a brain can see that this is what is happening.

I never thought America would become (or feel like we are in) another country. But we have to keep pushing forward, because that is what working people do. This is also what entrepreneurs do. If you come to a roadblock in life you just keep searching until you find another way. Don't ever give up.

If you find that your job slipping away look right away for something to fall back on. Don't wait until you lose that job. Believe in yourself at all times and continue to be the man or

∽

women God created you to be. Do not wait, I repeat, do not wait until government tells you what to do because that decision will be in their best interests, not yours. Don't get sucked into the dependency mode that they are hoping for. Sure, we are living in challenging times. But our parents and grandparents made it and can too. Like I said before, this is the land of opportunity and abundance so let's start or continue to act like it. Our financial situation is stressful, but we will pull through this. I know I will, and I know you will.

Right now we might not be as far ahead financially as we would like to be, but God is watching each and every one of you out there so keep the faith and stay on track. Keep working hard for you and your families. Keep putting food on the table like Mom and Daddy did.

Keep putting some money into the savings account and other places. (Never keep all of your money in one place.)

Keep things a little scattered in case something happens financially in America that could paralyze your access to money and impede financial survival for your family. In other words, don't keep all of your eggs in one basket.

If you are telling yourself that you don't have enough money to worry about, don't think that way. Remember, we have a dollar that is falling and it is only made of paper. China knows this. China stays involved in minerals, gold, and other financial avenues to secure themselves. We are borrowing too much money and this is taking us downhill. One slight, unexpected change and our financial system could be in even

ℒ

greater trouble. Our leaders like this insecurity even though it is crippling the average American.

Whatever you do be cautious about your money because at the end of the day it is *your* money. The government knows this is your money and they are starving for more of it. What better way to get it. They are scaring the hell of people and they know that it's working. But this will only work as long as you let it.

Everything is just another tax to build them up; just one more program and one more innocent American losing their life savings, or retirement.

Do your friends understand what is going on? Do they look at you and think you are crazy? Then, do you later hear through the grape vine that you are a racist? It is funny how people start treating you differently and look at you funny when you step outside of your comfort zone and start speaking out. Don't be afraid to speak out about our financial situation because, as you can tell, all the working people that once earned their keep are now losing it all through the socialistic policies of this administration.

Just remember that when you do decide to firmly speak out, that people will then start targeting you. Some people don't even want to build a business or work hard anymore because of the reverse psychology that our government has laid out. I know you are tired, but now is the time to catch that second wind and say, "NO MORE!"

The Working Man Fights for Right

We cannot let this disease consume our lives and the lives of our children. Washington thrives on crisis in this day and age so we have to start living our lives in forward gear instead of reverse. The more stimulus packages and the more government programs that come our way, the more our dollar keeps falling. And remember, the rest of the world would like nothing better than to see America fold.

The scary part is that our government knows that this is an opportunity for it to once again get even richer. Talks of a 'New World Order' is also officially in the mix. A global system is being built so get ready for it. There is an economic shift happening so be aware.

Remember what your parents taught you about finances and you will be fine. Always manage your life and family and your money the way you know best because in the end *you* make the financial decisions for your families and businesses, not the government. Take Charge!

CHAPTER 7

I Have One God and He Is Not Obama

I have a passion for God and doing the right things in life. Do you? I choose to pray whenever and wherever I choose. You don't always have to be in church to pray, but make it a point to be there if you can. If it wasn't for God I would not be here today. We can do all things through Christ who strengthens us. Stay true to God and you will be everything you ever wanted to be. You will be a successful person and a loving person, so keep the faith.

The Working Man Fights for Right

Our president has followers that pretty much worship him and that is okay right? Or is it? He practically walks on water in their eyes. Those people need to wake up and wake up fast. This is false hope coming from someone who is controlling a free country. Call me what you want to, but the truth will set you free. You see, a president can only do so much and there is only so much that he will do. If you get cut short, oh well.

What is the best health care plan in the world, bar none? Our Lord Jesus Christ. He is the answer to a suffering economy, illness, a troubled day, or huge disaster or any tragedy. My Savior gets me through anything and everything. A government program or talking to a government official is not the answer for anyone. I will pray to arrive at my decisions for my family and my country. You have to have faith in God, always, in good times and bad. When you put God first, anything is possible.

If you have a bad day—and Lord knows we have them now—or maybe an argument with your spouse or brother or sister, just say a prayer. My days are a whole lot sweeter when I look up at the clouds and take a deep breath, relax, and put God first again.

The reason I said that is because sometimes you may get side tracked in life. The devil enters your life and wants to destroy everything you did that day. No matter the time of day, the devil may pop up and try to guide you the wrong way. This is where God comes in. The key to beating the devil

❧

is that you have to let God come back into your life. You will know when you have turned away from him. He did not turn away from you, you turned away from him. Remember that God will never turn away from you.

When nothing goes right at work or at home and you think the world is going to end because you are pissed off (and you think everything you have done that day is crappy), think about this...

Settle down, and go sit alone for awhile before tearing into a family member for no reason. You very well may have a good reason to get angry, but your family may have not have been the cause of it. Always, and I mean always, turn your thoughts to the man upstairs.

You know as well as I do that when you finally are doing good in life, something or somebody always tries to steal your joy. Does this sound familiar? When people are doing the right thing and making the right decision for their business or family, what happens? The devil pops up again and tries to take away everything you worked for and achieved. Just remember there is always someone out there poised to tear you down.

These times we are living in will become harder as the days pass by. We need to keep working hard and invent new ideas for our businesses to stay afloat. We cannot let this government take over our lives. Continue to stay close to your kids and spouse, remembering that we cannot allow our kids to live in a corrupt nation. Our values, principles, and morals need to remain the foundation of this country and we must continue to stand firm each and every day.

This new America we live in now is just plain scary and it upsets me that one day I won't be here anymore to protect my family when God makes the call for me to come up and watch from above. This is why we have to do anything and everything in our own power now to prepare our kids for this new way of living. Everything won't change completely, but it may very well be different enough to matter. I will rest peacefully as I watch from Heaven because I did what I had to do to make my family's life easier, and to help them be prepared for the future.

We all have one leader and he is God. We have to continue to live a free American life in a God loving country. This is what America is all about. For every failure there is success. For every mistake there is a lesson learned. Have passion when you speak out. Enhance your desire to worship one God and be the messenger that spreads the gift of freedom across this nation.

We all have worked to build this country up. Don't allow the false hopes of getting your house paid for or of getting a free car from the president. God put us on this earth with duties and we have a responsibility to take care of ourselves and to be great individuals. You will still have to pay for your own fuel. You will have to pay your own bills. The president is not God and he will not erase your sorrows. (Perhaps there are some beverages you can buy that will drown your sorrows, but that is not a good road to take either.)

Some Americans need to realize that this so called change we have now isn't a brand new adult daycare center that just opened up. You will have to do some things on your own. I know the president looks good in his suits and talks with clarity; I do give him some credit. But just remember that he won't be able to pay down your debt when you want him to.

If you trip and fall he will not catch you. Whenever you buy a new car he will not allow it to run without fuel or oil in it. You will have to get up and take care of certain things.

What is the difference between President Obama and GOD?

OBAMA	GOD
Stressful.	Relaxing!
Scares me.	Welcomes me.
Will not save you from the fires of Hell.	God WILL save me.
Doesn't treat everyone equally.	All are equal in God's eyes.
Drains my bank account.	Unlimited access to money.
Doesn't like achievment from one person.	Notices achievements everyday!
Creates a rainy day.	Parts the clouds and let's the sun shine!
Forces programs down your throat.	Provides you with the knowledge to make your own decisions with your own brain.
Can walk on water? Almost.	He can!

I could go on and on and on. You pretty much get the picture. We all have one God and He is not the president.

We will get past these troubled times, we will. The Lord still works in mysterious ways. Everything happens for a

෨

reason, and there is a reason why this country is in this situation. I look at it like this; we have merely lost our way.

We have been consumed by things that don't matter — celebrities, expecting to receive something for nothing, video games, cell phones and texting and having to own the latest gadgets, and we are forgetting who we are. We are forgetting who our real creator is.

This is about our lives here. We must continue to stay close to our families and to God. We have to believe that we can pull through all of this. Pray for one another, and for yourself, that we will become the country we once were.

Sometimes during these hard days I cry. Believe it or not I do. Life gets me down and I really don't know how to feel or what to feel, and I wonder if I should get mad or just go somewhere and be by myself and think about the good American life.

Our country is going through some major changes right before our eyes and it is heart wrenching to see such a beautiful nation and prosperous nation become the equivalent of a second rate foreign country. We have a purpose here on earth and one of them is to keep America the way she was founded.

God help us to remember and exercise our core principles and values; the values that that you have instilled in each and every one of us. One president, whoever he is, (now, or 50 years from now) should not steer people in the wrong direction.

❧

My family is my inspiration. My wife and two children are the reason I do what I do. They are the reason I get up every morning and continue my hard working life here in the great USA. My children are who I worry about the most. No one knows where this country is really headed or whether we will be rich or poor. Your kids must get educated and be aware of their surroundings, but at the same time try and enjoy life to the fullest. What I mean is, they should still have fun but realize what is going on in the world around them.

Certain issues affect your job, your investments, your town, and sometimes your religion. And most of all, your family. A lot more people are involved in politics these days and that is good. But having said that, the ordinary man and woman need to stay more aware about their leaders .

No one will ever control or govern the choices of my family other than my family and me. God will also make choices for me and I will be at peace with those choices because He knows what is right. And He knows if America will still be America tomorrow. He will be the guidance I need and provide the strength to continue in a society that is currently very difficult to live in.

No one else will ever make my life any easier than our Lord. The people are really pulling together now and are becoming one. The people of this great country know what America needs. I can feel it, I can see it, and I can breathe freedom coming back.

The Working Man Fights for Right

୨୦

It took us this long to realize where this country was headed and now we have awakened and we will no longer go back to sleep. If you remain aware of your surroundings you will experience a movement unlike any you have ever seen before.

The secret to retaining our freedom is to stay focused on our surroundings and to stay on the offensive and be ready for anything that comes our way at all times. We will be the victor not the victim.

You will always succeed by the grace of God through your belief in him and the faith that you will be the most powerful person in the world. Not because of money, not because of fame, and not because of popularity, but because you have chosen to turn to God in your life. He will guide and protect you more than anybody on this earth. You need to remember that. Pray on that and your heart will be calm, quiet, and free from any discomfort you may have—politically, mentally, physically , or emotionally.

I "preach" to you today because Obama has had enough chances to do it so now I want mine.

- You do not need a political figure to show you the way.
- You do not need someone to force you, tell you, or make you do anything you do not want to do.
- You are in control of your own life.
- My only partner that will get me through is God.

❧

Yes, I have only one God and It is not Obama. I think I am going to go give my wife and kids a hug right now and thank the Lord for them. All I want is to have my family protected and to stay safe; that's all I really want anymore. Ask yourself what it is that you really want anymore.

Do you remember when Jesus spread the good news to everyone? Even back then people disagreed with his beliefs but he still pressed on and didn't worry about it.

I think it is our turn as freedom lovers in America to spread the good news of how our nation should really be run to keep it truly free. We have to speak out and take action on what we as Americans believe in and not be afraid to do that. I'm to the point that I'll do whatever I need to do because God is on my side, and no one will take that away from me.

Material things may be taken away from me but my love for my country and the passion that I have to allow myself to accept whatever happens proves that I am ready to do whatever it takes to set this country free again.

If we go back to horses and wagons and beans in a can then so be it. If I have to get back on my little blue tractor and break the ground for my family then that is exactly what I will do. Remember, we are all here temporarily. I know we want everything to be good and not have to bear a whole lot of stress in our lives, but now we have even more.

God wants us to be strong people now and even stronger tomorrow. That is why we have obstacles in our way every

The Working Man Fights for Right

ֆ

day. They happen when we least expect it or whenever things seem to be going smoothly. It seems as if something always happens to us along our life journeys. Up jumps the devil!

I remember when my daddy passed away in August of 1999. I thought my world was going to end. I was only twenty-two years old at the time. I had so much to tell him and to talk with him about. The only thing that got me through was God. It wasn't a president, it wasn't money, it wasn't alcohol either. It was the big man himself: God.

I did feel my dad giving me strength throughout his passing. I could feel it. The strength that he gave me was through the blessing of God. We have so much left to tell our loved ones and no matter how long they have been on this earth, their time here is never long enough.

The way I see things now is that I'll build my life not only thinking that Daddy's watching. I'll build it *knowing* that he's watching. That keeps me going because I told myself a long time ago that I can't see him, hug him, or shake his calloused hands, but I can show him what I can do and accomplish while I am still here on earth.

Our loved ones, believe it or not, are watching us and are beside us every day. They are here in spirit. And Lord, protect us and guide us back to a place where we can be free and not be forced to do things against our will.

Think about this chapter and never forget it.

CHAPTER 8

Is This What Our Politicians Really Do? And Ruminations on Our Military

Have you ever wondered why people on the left do not like the capitalists and rich people on the right? It's strange because many on the left are some of the richest people in America. Politicians can sit there and say we have to do this and have to do that but who are the ones making all the money? Our leaders are. So with that being said, let's talk about what is going on now. And yes, since he is on the television so much and gives so

ॐ

many speeches, who better to talk about than the one and only Barack Obama.

He wanted change for America and that is what he got. People voted for change and that is what we also got. I looked in my cookie jar yesterday and what did I get? A lot less change. A couple of quarters, a dime, and three nickels. I love this new era of change, don't you?

Politicians do lie a lot and most of the time they get away with it. Mister Tax Cheat himself, former Secretary of the Treasury, Timothy Geithner, started the first term with our mighty president and is now making more money than ever since he left after his former boss' first term to become a banker in the private sector.

The people would like to know how lives with himself doing business the wrong way and avoids financial scandal, but when ordinary Americans make an honest mistake they get thrown in jail or prison. Why are our so called leaders somehow better than everyone else?

The campaign trail is one of the biggest scams in the country. They tell people one thing just to win and after all is said and done they do the exact opposite. I have to hand it to our president, he never stopped campaigning until after he was sworn in for his second term.

———————

❧

For the most part Obama's policies are for the birds. If you think about it they only benefit the government and their own pockets.

The working man has a tough time living in these types of conditions. A lot of people who thought everything would be fine are now finding out that things are not at all what they voted for. This is too much control and too much money going where it shouldn't. Our politicians need to listen to the people and admit deep down that something isn't right.

When disagrees with a policy on the president's agenda, that shouldn't be a punishable situation. It's called freedom of speech and the freedom to protest in America. The people want the truth and they are not getting it. The people want real answers and not some speech that shames the individual for speaking their mind. Say what you mean, and mean what you say, but it's probably a little too late for that, Mr. President.

The people are only going to take so much and then you will have to listen to us. Now that you've won a second term it's time to saddle up and run this country the right way. I hope God gives you the strength to help this country because you need something to fix this, and I don't mean that you get to sit down and have a beer with someone to solve a problem.

These issues affect real lives here. Just be a real president, not someone who thrives on crises every day. Some people would say, "Oh get over it, you lost we won." But it makes you wonder who you voted for. Is he just another politician

ዒ

being unfaithful to the people once again? So far, I say the answer is yes.

Do we know who our politicians really are, and are they really capable of leading a free country?

Do they really have an interest in our issues this country faces? Or are they just control freaks who thrive on Washington power, like some leaders do? I think I hit the nail on the head with that one.

You see, when you have a chance to make a lot of money some people take advantage of others for their own personal gain. This kind of activity is very dangerous to a country's future, especially when the government has access to the printing machine that make more dollars—dollars that the American people seldom know where the government intends to spend it. The government doesn't care about the people so why should it care about where the dollars are spent? To the government, dollars are like Doritos... They'll make more!

This particular government believes in taking from someone who has earned money and then giving it to another who didn't do a damn thing to get it.

I may be repeating myself but this subject is worth repeating because some Americans haven't gotten it through their heads yet. It is simply that the rich are getting taxed to pay for the people who didn't work for it.

I personally believe that if you worked longer hours or worked harder, or let's say you like to take more risks than

❧

others—like entrepreneurs—it doesn't give a politician the right to tax achievers (better known as the working man) and pass it on to someone else. This is just another crooked move by a control hungry politician who's messing with individual private lives across the country.

How can a politician do this to the people who voted them in and sleep like a baby at night?

How can you not do something to stop this crisis in its tracks? The answer: This administration feeds on the word crisis, and when all is said and done the American people may never know who we are truly voting for. Stop dictating our lives, this is America and the people will keep it that way just fine. In the end you will see that it is the people who actually run this country.

Ultimately the people will prevail over any politician so why don't you politicians just accept the fact and do the peoples' work. It's why we gave you the job. Now do the work we expect from you, and you'll do well.

Now excuse me while I go make me a Crown and Coke. Can I still do that? It's what the politicians do, isn't it? Does anyone else want one? I have an endless supply just like the government does!

Have you ever worked and concentrated on something during the day and thought about our country when suddenly tears began to run down your face? Were you so frustrated with everything, worried about you, your kids, your spouse, job, and even your future? Maybe you were driving that nail in that two by four piece of lumber and found yourself just hitting and hitting it. Or you were digging that hole along a new fence or water line and you tossed that shovel on the ground in anger and asked yourself, "Why do we need shovel ready jobs when all we do is have a shovel in our hands all day anyway?"

I mean, what good is it to have a temporary program that will help for a little but doesn't offer any stability? We have plenty of shovel ready jobs down in Texas already. And the best thing about that is we do not have to tax everyone to create those jobs.

We have fences, power line companies, gravel roads, and plenty of auction rings, and horse barns. So if anyone from Washington wants a shovel-ready job, just come on down to Texas. We'll help ya'll out with that and the Working Man will hold on to his money a little longer.

How about this one: You can be praying in Church or just be praying at your job or at home when out of the blue something moves you the tears flow again. It's a sign of your passion and your belief that something isn't right in our world. You have worked so hard to get to where you're at and it seems like everything just slips farther away. I have those days too.

Our drive to be who we want to be is being tested and we're being tested like no other time before. Everything the working man has built is slowly disappearing. Are you upset

॰ৡ

about this? Especially when someone just sits behind a desk all day and tells you what to do.

I startled my wife one day when I was going on and on about our country and I was really getting passionate. I was also upset and stressed over some other issues that were being forced upon us. She slowly but surely calmed me down. It's just that I love my country and I don't want everything I have worked so hard for go to the dogs. Me and a lot of other hard working people have done so much to provide for their future. And now to see America changing in the wrong way is so hard to swallow.

To have a desire to build a business or to continue to work for the same company for a quarter of century is a milestone in a lot of peoples' lives. This can only come from dedication, determination and effective skills in the work force. This defines the working American.

We can get discouraged at times but if we didn't life would be too easy. Life is a journey. Some days are better than others. Your job is to be the American God created you to be.

Never be afraid to ask questions. Here's some for The Big Man.

Q. What country did you think you were in when you ran for President?

The Working Man Fights for Right

త

Q. Do you really want the achiever to now live poor because you now have full control?

Q. Would you want to be in Afghanistan in the middle of a war and not have enough soldiers on the ground to help you out?

These are really good questions and they are truly about our nation. Our country was built on freedom and our lives right now are truly not free. George W. Bush: bet you like him a little better now, don'tcha?

I think a lot of people are intimidated by our leaders. Yes, they run in higher circles than the ordinary American does, but that doesn't mean they are better than we are. A baseball coach once told me before a game, "Don't be intimidated by the other team, they put their pants on one leg at a time just like you do." There's some truth to that; if there wasn't then those other players would have to jump into mid-air and slide their legs inside their pants pretty damn quick.

I have another question: How rich do you really have to get before you start leaving the working man alone, Mr. President? When we voted we just wanted a president that would be for the people, not just about his political gains. People wanted change, but man, what the hell happened? I know you like to make history every time you are on the television but I've lost count of how many times you have been on television.

❧

I love America, do you?

I love it when our military kicks other countries asses for the right reasons, so why do you have a problem with that?

Why do you have to apologize for America's accomplishments? You know, when you apologize for us winning a war, and you really wished we would have lost, that is a slap in all of our soldiers' faces. I do not know if you realize it or not but you are hurting yourself.

Mr. President, we have shovel-ready jobs down here in Texas and Texans did not have to tax the whole nation to get them. We have fences to be built and also mended. We have foundations that we are pouring as we speak because we don't give a damn about the government. We will build and rebuild whenever we want.

Our economy down here is not in a crisis like you're hoping it would be. Do you love a crisis ? It seems to a lot of us that you do because you are taking advantage of people more often than not with your government scares. Can you sleep at night ? If so, tell everyone your secret.

How did you master the ability to portray such a calm and collected attitude when our country is in so much stress financially and economically? Oh that's right, the working people of this nation just keep making you richer. I can't believe I forgot about that.

I may sound like a butt, but all of this is true and it affects the nation I dearly love. Mr. President, could you pass me that shot glass over there? Or perhaps we could talk about our disagreements in Margaritaville so you can hear me tell you that it's my own damn fault.

I love this country and we Americans are not going to let it slip away so easily, and not without a fight. This book is all about individual freedom, and freedom for our country. The people intend to keep it that way by any means necessary. We will be ready to rebuild this country whenever you are so just let us know and we will be behind you one-hundred percent.

How is it that when you talk to the United Nations you are God's gift to the world while you openly continue to tear down my country? You not only lie to us, you lie to the rest of the world.

Why not just bring home the troops because you don't have the drive or honor to do anything to help them anyway. We will stay the superpower of the world but in the meantime someone needs to take the microphone away from you. You are not President of the World and you don't seem to be in our country, either. The ordinary American is still searching for that one person to serve in the Oval Office in an honorable way while still guarding America's interests at home and abroad.

We will not change the climate or the planet and the land will not go anywhere and at the same time you blame America for it. Mr. President, tell me another one.

You were not voted in for this kind of destruction so stop blaming us for everything. How does this make you feel when you listen to yourself especially when you are supposed to be

❧

the leader? If our country is so bad in your eyes then why did you even want to be the president? Because what you want to do is not the America that America knows, and Americans will not stand for someone that is for foreign countries more than their own. Please stop apologizing for our actions in the world; just stop, just stop.

How did you pull off winning the Nobel Peace Prize when you were president for only twelve days?

Do I get a refund for your loss in Copenhagen on the Olympic issue or do I just get a complimentary can of Copenhagen? I could have used some of the money that fueled *Air Force One* and bought some more hay for my cattle and deer. Do I sound arrogant to you? I mean, you have said yourself that America is a country that is arrogant. Where will your next beer summit be?

When we have beer summits in Texas we sit around a campfire with a cooler in the back of the truck. If you ever want to find us we will be way back in the back woods enjoying God's great land. We'll have our radio cranking—not to Rush Limbaugh, but to *A Country Boy Can Survive*.

Are we ever going to see our refund checks from the stimulus packages? I mean, if the companies failed, even after you had to sign the destruction of America bill, then the individuals want their money back.

This is all the time I have for now because I have some work to do. So, Mr. President, I guess we'll talk later. Oh, one more thing: Don't be so forceful with everything when you

The Working Man Fights for Right

ॐ

talk to the American people because you have to remember that WE THE PEOPLE have and will always get the last word. Our time is coming and your time is going.

One more thing, Mr. President. How is it that your buddy George W. Bush knew how to handle personal pressure and you don't? What I mean is that whenever you get criticized you just shut down a company or you get people that are so-called officials to go out and hunt us down. At the same time there are terrorists and other world leaders that hate our guts, and then you turn around and act like their friend. I just can't get this through this soon-to-be-bald head of mine. I thought you were our leader. I thought we were going to see some change; change for the people, not the government.

If you want to level the playing field so bad, then why are you richer than me? I mean, you live in The White House. If I want a white house I'll have to paint it white and then sit back and watch my taxes go up because I made some improvements. In return for this my money goes back to Washington.

That is not even close to being a level playing field. If you have *Air Force One*, then we all should get an *Air Force One* to fly around in. Even though some of us don't have our pilots' license, I still want one. That is pretty much how it works now, right? Some people get things that aren't even theirs in this new era of redistribution of wealth, so there you have it.

I have to go now; the Tax Man Cometh. God help us all.

❧

Earlier I mentioned our dear soldiers and how they don't have a fair shake under the Obama regime. What are our soldiers really fighting for? You know, I am really starting to wonder about our soldiers. Our only true protection from the enemy is our military.

Our brave men and women on the front lines fight for you and me every day of our lives. As the days pass I wonder what are our soldiers really fighting for? These trained military professionals fight and risk their lives and they don't even know you. Have you ever stopped to think about that? They have one thing on their mind and it is freedom.

Our military has protected countries around the world and here at home since its inception back in the 1700s. We have come to the aid of countries some people haven't even heard of. So how can a superpower like the USA—because we still are in my eyes—experience so much turmoil on our own soil?

After having President Bush as our leader—someone who offered so much encouragement, had endurance, and a love for America and the military—why did we choose to succumb to an administration that is so anti-American?

President Bush did not tear down the country. If we needed more troops they were deployed as needed. What is happening to our military now is very scary for our soldiers who need so much more help. Let's avoid another Vietnam. Let's enjoy a true victory and then come home.

The Working Man Fights for Right

This president we have now is deaf to the American voice. Other countries seem more important, their problems seem to come first, and our soldiers now come last even when it comes to increasing forces where needed. How do you think that makes a soldier feel?

How do you think a father feels about his son out there in the war zone who cannot get help from what should the best-run military headquarters in the world? This is immoral and unthinkable to us as a common sense people. Let's face it, some people don't appreciate someone like me running down their president and I fully understand that. But a lot of countries hate our guts and there has to be a reason for that. I guess if I was trying to be bigger, smarter, and more dominant and have everyone flock to my country , I'd be pissed off too.

I am very proud of my country, even long before Michele Obama said so. Can you believe it? The government is involved with too many things here at home.

Our soldiers want to come home to a free nation, like it was when they left to go fight for freedom somewhere 6,000 miles away. Is that too much to ask? Someone needs to be held accountable for these actions against Americans.

When a soldier puts his boots on, the helmet, the backpacks, and their gun, that soldier's mindset is to keep his or her country free and return home

A soldier has determination like none other. The liberty they fight for are still the same as it always was. We were free when we first established this great nation, and we have to make sure that we stay free today. It's our duty as Americans.

Put yourself into the shoes of a soldier. When that soldier is on the battle field and looks one more time at a picture of his baby daughter or baby boy, or his wife or her husband back home, isn't the thought of them never coming home again heart wrenching?

We also need to keep our borders safe and secure. Cut the bull crap and let's get the job done. And I have another question: Why is it that when the USA needs to pursue a problem it's like, "Oh no!" But when another country has a problem they just jump all over it. Let our soldiers be soldiers and let them get the job done, and then allow them to come home with a victory.

It's a slap in the face of our military when people bitch about a war and don't even realize who they're talking about. It's like, "Oh well, our soldiers just lost their lives for nothing."

The lack of respect shown in this country is also very high, from the president disrespecting and ignoring the wishes of our sergeant's in the field. Maybe our president needs to take a few lessons from Bush. At least Bush had the balls to stand up for our country. He stood firm in his belief of our country.

Our previous president knows the difference between a dictator and a true president. We now have a president who agrees with dictators and murderers. And our soldiers are supposed to be pumped up about that?

The Working Man Fights for Right

We need a leader that is for the military and for freedom. Our president has forgotten some things about our great nation. We, the USA, have footed the bill for damn near the whole planet.

We have fed the hungry, protected the weak, and still to this day are protecting our country without a distraction from someone who isn't for freedom. When Obama wants to cut the defenses and bring home soldiers when the job isn't done yet, or just to protect his own political agenda, that is wrong! Our soldiers need to know that we are truly behind them. They need to know that every minute of every day they are fighting for the best country in the world, for their kids, their families, and their friends. But mostly they fight for us; they fight for people they will never know.

If we dismantle our military get ready for fireworks in the streets, chains and multiple locks on our yard gates. We will not even be able to go the store without "Dirty Harry" strapped on us.

Who wants to live like that? Is this all our soldiers are fighting for? I certainly hope not, but look where this country is headed. This agreeing to and being on the same level as another country run by a dictator is not going to work for the true Americans here at home.

America needs to get back to the basics in life. We need to really think about the word 'change'. That's the word that is dismantling this nation every day. Change is nothing more than a sales pitch that screwed the American people. Some

✍

voted for it, and what happened? America changed into the country that one man wanted, not the change that the people wanted. We refuse to be punished for our hard work and the people will not tolerate this kind of behavior much longer.

Our borders are a serious problem, not only in Texas but all the way around the U.S. The borders breed danger but where is all the reinforcement? Instead of building government into a bigger behemoth over health care, why not take some of that money that was supposed to go to A.C.O.R.N. and put it into protecting our borders? That thought took half a brain.

The bottom line is to stop illegals from doing more damage to this country, and other sinister threats to us. If you are from some third world mess of a country and want to come over to America, do it the right way. Even though the right way has been lost just do it anyway and maybe things would not be so distorted in America. We need more support on our borders, not more questions.

We have to let our soldiers know that we have everything under control here at home. We have to stay positive on our home land so our soldiers can keep a positive mindset abroad. Many of us didn't ask for this kind of transformation, but we got it. And now we have to get out of it.

When people call some conservatives and Tea Party people hate mongers, know that all these right wing people want is their freedom back. When the left and other

സം

organizations ridicule the true Americans like Glenn Beck, Rush Limbaugh, and Sean Hannity, those people need to step back and listen for about thirty seconds and they could perhaps learn why those three guys love this country so much. With that being said, would you ever approach a soldier and say the same things you tell the ordinary American? To all the people who are going up to the soccer moms, single moms, veterans, our grandparents and dads, why not go up to a soldier and say that to his or her face?

That soldier is putting life on the line for you and me. That soldier deserves respect from every American. It's always easier to talk about it but to actually get a job done is a whole other ball game.

You also have to remember that our soldiers are fighting for everyone, not just one family or one person. They have no agenda. I pray every day that our president will cease to dismantling our military anymore than he has.

Meanwhile, the hate aimed at the conservatives and the Tea Party needs to stop and some of these freedom critics need to gear up and go out into the desert and find out what it really feels like to do some real work for a change. Sit down with a soldier and find out what it's all about. Ask questions, I did.

Just remember that we need to keep our country safe and remain a place that our soldiers want to come back home to. And that means keeping it free. After all, they are fighting for freedom right so they should at least enjoy some of what they

❧

are fighting for. And as for our president not wanting to be first in the world (and stay there), what the hell is that all about? These other (mostly Muslim) countries are jumping with joy; their dreams have come true at the words of our president.

Listen up, Mr. President: America is not sorry, America is not arrogant, and America is not going to bow down to anybody who is dictatorially controlling their countries.

America is confident, proud, and is still striving to stay the best in spite of you. That is not to arrogant to me.

The way I see it is when you try and make your way to the top, that's one thing. But the one that has always stayed at the top and is a shining beacon to the rest of the world is the United States of America. It really is that cut and dried, and now it's time for you to fish or cut bait, Mr. Obama. Are you hearing me?

A lot of Americans have had family members in the military and each of these service men and women knew what it took to stay free. They worked hard in the past just as they are today. It means a lot to have a family member that fought in a war for our freedom. We would not be enjoying the lives we have if it wasn't for grandpa or mom or dad or even granny. We have a lot to be thankful for today. Even in these troubled times, we still are blessed dearly from God above.

My grandfather fault in World War II. I never got a lot of history out of him because I was too young to really realize (and appreciate) that this was a   golden opportunity to

୬

capture some history from a true soldier. Although he did tell me that he had to fight "them damn Japanese!"

He was stationed in the Philippines. The bullets were flying, bombs going off around him, so how did he make it back home? I don't know. Grandpa said, "Them bullets were just hitting my helmet, tink, tink, tink."

A little later on I asked him, "Grandpa, what did you eat?" He replied, "Well, we ate some beans in a can. We didn't have a home cooked meal for the most part."

"You had to eat out of a can?" I replied.

"When you have only so much to work with you'll get hungry and find a way to survive, and you just make the best of it," he told me.

I also remember him talking about a big python snake crawling around, and the occasional wild hog. His main concern was to get back home to Granny.

The next soldier in my family that gave his all for our country would be my dad. Grandpa Filip's son, Edward J. Filip, fought in Vietnam. We all remember that one don't we? Here again, I was kind of young, but I did squeeze out some answers from Dad. He really didn't want to say much about it; I could tell as a young boy that it bothered him to talk about it

"Did you fly in a helicopter when you were in the Army?" I asked him, tentatively.

"Yes I did, I flew in a big Chinook. We called 'em Snooks. It has two big propellers and it was solid green."

"What kind of gun did you have?" I asked him.

"An M-14 and M-60 machine gun."

He was a man of few words most of the time, and especially when I brought up the subject of his military days. It was not a very happy subject for him to talk about.

The Boeing CH-47 Chinook Helicopter. Of the nearly 750 Chinooks flown during the Vietnam War, about 200 were lost in combat or operational accidents.

Then I asked him The Big One.

"When you were in the Army did you ever kill anyone ?"

Oh boy, that did not go over well. Dad got very quiet and all he did was slowly nod his head. He never said it out loud to me, just a barely perceptible affirmative nod. I did manage to ask him one more question.

"Dad," I asked sheepishly, "did you lose any of your buddies in the war?"

The Working Man Fights for Right

He nodded again. It was reverent.

After that I just never really brought it up anymore. I was young but I had seen firsthand the hurt in his eyes. It pained him to talk about it so I finally let it go. I've since lost my chance to learn any more history from my dad because cancer took him from me in August of 1999. The man had a lot of information in his head but I was too young to figure out how to approach him again after our last talk.

That's him (above) in Vietnam. I call that a grass hut. I'm sure it's called something else, but that is what I call it. How about we throw some people who don't like freedom into the jungles of Vietnam. Do you think they would survive? NOPE!

To the right is another picture of him holding his gun. Study this picture if you can. I am sure some will find this photo a little tough to look at because of the memories it evokes. His helmet, the gun, the boots. That gun was his buddy. He never put it down in those conditions. These pictures are very touching to those who have served in Vietnam. There were a lot of lives lost in that particular war. I imagine a soldier with ammo hanging around his neck in the middle of a steamy and insect-infested jungle fighting for his life. I see my dad.

Washington needs to take a close look at these pictures. He sacrificed for us and for his buddies and I'm sure you probably know someone who has done the same

To me my grandpa and dad are my heroes. I never gave it a thought when I was young , but I sure do now.

Our families mean the most to us, more than any amount of money or more than any America haters across the world. Can you feel my sadness? Can you feel my anger? Can you feel how much I love this country?

The Working Man Fights for Right

I Love you Grandpa, and I Love you Dad. Thanks so much for your hard work and all that you have done for me and for our country.

CHAPTER 9

A Post-9/11 World

Have you forgotten 9/11? Disturbingly, some have or just really don't worry about it anymore. 2,752 American's were stolen from us and 343 firefighters and police officers were struck down as well. If this didn't get your attention, then nothing will.

What in the hell happened that day? If this wasn't an act of war then you tell me what is? This was the real wakeup call for us and the world. It's time for our own president to wake

⎯⎯

up. Our soldiers are in harm's way every day—especially after 9/11.

Someone needs to lead this country with freedom at the top of the list because what we have now, well, you can see where we and our soldiers are at. God, please be with our soldiers, someone has to.

How can someone be a leader of the USA and not see the big picture? Whenever you have a tragedy like September 11, 2001, you have to have a bigger vision concerning our problems and standing threats.

When the planes hit the World Trade Center buildings our lives were forever changed by terrorists. Flights 93, 77, 175, and 11, will forever remain in our hearts and prayers. Our world changed forever that day

From the airliner that hit the Pentagon to the plane in the Pennsylvania field, we became a truly united nation. We cannot forget that day. Our own people jumping out of windows perched one-hundred floors in the Manhattan skies and calling their loved ones for the last time. People no different than you and me running for their lives, chased by toxic dust and debris clouds that enveloped them in terror. Why is it so hard for our leadership to see our desire, drive, and determination to stay free?

There were kids barely out of high school from every town across this country willing to risk their lives the moment it happened. They just enlisting into the military as soon as possible. Does this president we have now reflect this drive?

We had that from President George W. Bush. Where the hell is it now? I think our mothers and fathers deserve an explanation from our leaders.

What is the problem with finishing a war with people who are shooting at innocent civilians and hijacking us for no damn reason? You want to level the playing field, well your playing the wrong game with the American people. If you choose to level the playing field and throw out the word freedom, then what is it all for?

If you want America to be the same as Iran, Iraq, and Pakistan, and all of the other countries that hate us, then you really have no choice but to bring home every soldier that is fighting for freedom (and mainly our freedom). You cannot have it both ways.

I still cannot find any love of freedom in your eyes Mr. President. Our Government needs to read the Constitution and wake up. It's one thing when you get caught doing something and not realize it and then you correct it. But when you are caught doing something, and you know it's wrong, you can't keep doing it. For example: taking over free markets, running profitable businesses in the ground, squeezing the life out of our military, or doing other things instead of prioritizing your agenda to reflect America First.

I can't say this enough: Our freedom is under attack and now the war on freedom has landed on the doorsteps of every American. Wake up!

The Working Man Fights for Right

☙

America is a nation that is always continuing and winning the fight for Freedom. After 9/11 we were all forced to make changes in our lives. America was forced to again be the country she really was; America experienced a wakeup call.

Our country was the dominant one in the world, and today she still is. The terrorists did one thing: they woke us up. Now we just need to have a leader that will follow up with all of this and show the world that we will not back down to anybody. We cannot afford to level the playing field and expect better results in our individual safety and security twelve years later. It is a long and tiresome battle to stay free and to stay safe here on our own soil. Just remember one thing: anything worth fighting for and worth saving doesn't come easy.

Our families are at stake here. Our freedom is at stake here. People are tired. People want their kids back home. We either unleash the military and let them do their job to the fullest or bring them home. I know one thing. We have to ask God to help give our generals and soldiers the strength to pull through this rough time.

Our president made time a few years back to talk about the Olympics in Copenhagen while our soldiers were being killed. Michele Obama, your trips around the world are not even close to a sacrifice when you sit next to an American soldier. I have an idea. Why don't you help the children of the dead soldiers and explain to them why they died? What the hell is happening to us in this country?

❧

How do the disabled feel, these men and women who still have dreams of bombs going off in their heads? The nights of waking up in a cold sweat and sometimes hollering out to their buddies, or mom or dad. Tears running down their faces in distrust and disgust from trying to win a war half way around the world.

To come home with one leg or one arm is terrifying. To have a burned face forever and never again have the appearance you once had. Imagine getting off the plane to see your wife and kids for the first time, and your little girl sees her daddy in a wheel chair. When he left he was walking around like everyone else. Please Mr. President, listen to the people of this country and step up and protect our sons and daughters and never forget our veterans.

The feelings towards our country are strong. We have a passionate anger to do good in our lives. When I say anger, I mean we are so ready to do better than this and we are fed up with the way things are going. And it seems now that we just have to pursue our expectations with desire and anger. People are frustrated and will push forward even more because this way isn't going to cut it! I fully understand that our soldiers have to listen to our Commander-in-Chief, but we have to be reasonable about our world here. We have to use some common sense.

Do you know how a fighter gets when he is preparing for a fight? He is getting warmed up and he is focusing on his one objective: to win the fight. He is focusing on the ring and what to do to beat his opponent. Who feels like this now? A soldier? A soccer mom? Or maybe a father who has just lost his wife to cancer? I could name a million people who have the urge to come out of their shells right now and start taking this country back. I am with you, America. I see, feel, and I am experiencing what you are. Our country is under attack and the enemy is here on our own soil. The enemy is ignorance about what we are really about.

Our soldiers deserve better than this. Our soldiers deserve some answers. Why haven't the World Trade Center buildings been rebuilt yet? What is the hold up? This is America, isn't it? Let's rebuild and not look back. We are a country that knows how to do things. We went to the moon multiple times with computers that aren't as good as the one I am writing this book on. We have this in us as Americans. We owe this to all of the people who died on 9/11.

We will not be silenced by fear or by not speaking our minds. We need to serve our own people a lot more than we serve everyone else in the world. You have to continue to protect our soil, Mr. President, and by all means stand proud to be an American.

The apology tour of the past five years needs to stop. This is weakening our ability to protect ourselves. You need to apologize for playing golf and laughing everything off, while our soldiers are dying. Why cut defenses, as much as some countries hate us? Do you really think they will lay down their guns and nuclear forces? I think not. They may say they will,

❧

but don't let your guard down America. Can I say North Korea and those blasted Iranians?

I have also talked to another soldier here in Texas about the Iraq War. He is a co-worker of mine and a good friend. We both feel that the situation in Afghanistan is pretty sad. Especially when it is obvious that we need help over there and Washington doesn't, in my opinion, really care. The so-called public servants in Washington only care about themselves and they know it.

The first question I asked my friend (an Army sergeant) was, "How did you feel when you had to leave your family to go to war in Iraq?"

"Sad," he replied. One simple word that tells the truth, and nothing but the truth. I mean, what soldier would feel any different? He knew what he had to do and he did it. I went on to ask him another question.

"Did you ever have to shoot anyone while over there?"

"No," he said. I couldn't even imagine if you had to. Like I said, one simple word that can tell you a world of information. I might add that my friend was in the Army National Guard for five years and also has been in the Army Reserves for sixteen years. He is also a Texan.

As I thought about what to ask him next, I imagined my family for a moment and wondered how it would feel being gone for so long without a hug or a kiss from my wife and kids. When you can't even toss a ball with your son or watch your daughter cheer at the junior high football game.

The Working Man Fights for Right

§

Things are really different in a soldier's life. So then I ask, "What did you think about when you had some quiet moments sometimes? About your family? Or were you scared for your family and did you think you were coming back home or not?"

He replied, "I thought about my family and I usually phoned them up to talk as much as I could." That is what I would do. I talk too much, so I guess I'd be on the phone all the time.

It is amazing what you can learn by asking a soldier a few questions. If they haven't talked to a real, true soldier here in America, I just wanted the American people to realize what they are missing. It will make you feel so much different than you felt before about our country. Their answers will move you like nothing else. When you look into a soldier's eyes, you can see the desire, the determination, and the love in their voice when they talk to you about their experiences of fighting for the freedom that you and I can sometimes take for granted.

The next question I asked my friend was, "What was the feeling like, to actually fight in a war for yours and our freedom?"

The soldier answered, "I was proud I was doing something good for my country." He said he was proud for _doing_ something.

America, that is just it. Don't sit on the sidelines and wonder what will happen tomorrow. Don't say, "Well the government will take care of me."

No it won't. The Working Man and the soldier will. But if the government keeps this up, the Working Man will refuse to foot the bill for those who don't do anything. Because once the government destroys our military and the Working Man, we all lose.

My next question was, "Do some people here in America have a lot to be thankful for?"

He then replied, "I feel we have a lot to be thankful for in America, because not every country has the freedom we do."

Must we read anymore? Did you just read that answer? Let me repeat it, *I feel we have a lot to be thankful for in America, not every country has the FREEDOM WE DO.*

If only everyone felt this way, government would not be in our way. This is what America is all about. We have to believe that we are and can stay free forever in this country. I have been moved greatly by all of this. We are in the best country ever and we were built by God.

I thought a little more and felt I just had to ask this one. Hang on to your hats.

Do you think the President of The United States of America is *for* our military defenses or not?

He replied, "No."

"Have people under estimated 9/11, and have some forgotten about it?"

"Yes," he said. "Certain people don't believe in war until something bad happens here in America."

The Working Man Fights for Right

୨

So does that mean that we are we going to sit back and roll over to every terrorist and every country that hates us until another American building is blown up? Are we going to watch planes try to fly back into the Pentagon, or The White House? And only then will we decide to go to war with these evil freedom haters? It will be too late, and you know what? The same people who might not believe in war will be the same ones complaining that we failed to protect ourselves enough.

And maybe they will blame former president George W. Bush. You know why? Because That is all the current government knows how to do. They have blamed the auto companies, the Working Man for keeping what he has earned, and the greedy capitalist. But the Government can capitalize on our money and not miss a beat. Everything this country has been built on is under assault and we are the biggest targets for protecting our own country.

George W. Bush meant it when he said he will hunt down and find anyone who harbors any terrorist or is a threat to this country. That is a leader who cared about his country. He cared about the soldier. He cared about you. Of course everyone didn't like his policies either, but under his leadership he made me feel like a proud American.

It is easy to pass the blame onto someone else. It is easy to just curl up in a ball and hate everything around you. It is also easy to not take responsibility. Just because there were some kinks in the job, doesn't mean you have to blame the other

❧

guy. Every president gets the leftovers, and every president should be strong enough to handle the list of things a president has to do, or they should have never run for the job in the first place.

We have to protect our country no matter what. We live in a rough and scary world. Some may not like war, but I truly believe that if you want your life to stay the way it is, then we will have to sacrifice our lives to stay free. We have to keep our country strong and that means we have to be strong abroad also. Freedom doesn't come free. We as civilians know that.

Our hands may have to get dirty some days in order to get a job done. I thank the soldiers again for their hard work and dedication in protecting our country. The soldiers put themselves in the line of fire every day for you and me.

Think about this chapter, and really think about what we are doing here in America. Then ask yourself what our soldiers are really fighting for? You might want your voice to be heard after you give that some thought. Remember, every vote still counts. And right now every voice counts. Not tomorrow, not next week, not next year, but right now. Speak up and we will continue to be One Nation, Under God, Indivisible, with Liberty and Justice for All.

Make your voice heard.

CHAPTER 10

My America, Your America

You are about to read some of the most beautiful words ever written. They are inspirational in every sense of the word, and they are as true and relevant today as they were when they were first given to the American people.

The Gettysburg Address

Four score and seven years ago our fathers brought forth upon this continent, a new nation, conceived in liberty, and dedicated to the proposition that all men are created equal.

❧

Now we are engaged in a great civil war, testing whether that nation, or any nation so conceived and so dedicated, can long endure. We are met on a great battlefield of that war. We have come to dedicate a portion of that field, as a final resting place for those who here gave their lives that this nation might live. It is altogether fitting and proper that we should do this.

But in a larger sense, we cannot dedicate, we cannot consecrate, we cannot hallow this ground. The brave men, living and dead, who struggled here, have consecrated it, far above our poor power to add or detract. The world will little note, nor long remember what we say here, but it can never forget what they did here. It is for us, the living, rather to be dedicated here to the unfinished work which they who fought here have thus far so nobly advanced.

It is rather for us to be here dedicated to the great task remaining before us, that from these honored dead we take increased devotion to that cause for which they gave the last full measure of devotion; that we here highly resolve that these dead shall not have died in vain; that this nation, under God, shall have a new birth of freedom, and that this government of the people, by the people, and for the people shall not perish from this earth.

The Preamble to The Bill of Rights

C ongress of the United States begun and held at the City of New~York, on Wednesday the fourth of March, one thousand seven hundred and eighty nine.

THE Conventions of a number of the States, having at the time of their adopting the Constitution, expressed a desire, in order to prevent misconstruction or abuse of its powers, that further declaratory and restrictive clauses should be added: And as extending the ground of public confidence in the Government, will best ensure the beneficent ends of its institution.

RESOLVED by the Senate and House of Representatives of the United States of America, in Congress assembled, two thirds of both Houses concurring, that the following Articles be proposed to the Legislatures of the several States, as amendments to the Constitution of the United States, all, or any of which Articles, when ratified by three fourths of the said Legislatures, to be valid to all intents and purposes, as part of the said Constitution; viz.

ARTICLES in addition to, and Amendment of the Constitution of the United States of America, proposed by Congress, and ratified by the Legislatures of the several States, pursuant to the fifth Article of the original Constitution.

Think about who wrote these words and the spirit in which they were written. Is it too much to expect the same eloquence and belief in the American people from our lawmakers today?

While in no way an equal to the writers and framers of our Constitution, I did write to the people of South Texas in a letter to the editor of our local newspaper. (Don't forget, you have the ability to do the same thing. So do it!)

America, you know a lot of changes are going on around us and it is becoming a cancer and spreading fast. Maybe this will help and encourage you to always remember we will succeed and it really does start with YOU.

We have to turn back to our principles and values. Our country has run off the road. Let's agree to keep it strong. Maybe I can encourage you to stay positive in your life and move forward. Keep working hard keeping

The Working Man Fights for Right

God first in your life to lead the way. Even with all of these strings starting to tie down our freedoms right before our eyes, you have to stay focused on the right choices to make. One thing I try to do is to encourage my kids to do the best they can and talk to them every day to keep them on the straight and narrow.

There is a lot of negativity going on around us, and this makes it even harder to stay positive in this day and age. In other words, we cannot allow our kids to settle for what someone else wants us to settle for. You have to have the mindset of being and staying positive.

Yes, there are obstacles, but stay focused and you will succeed. There is an assault against our freedoms in this country. You cannot build an abundant life with regulation after regulation. The freedom to build and structure a positive outlook on life is being destroyed. The strings are getting longer and longer and they are stretching across the land, and you and I have to cut them.

The more strings on businesses mean less businesses and less profits, and more negativity occurs because of this. Sacrificing by paying higher taxes and seeing the redistribution of wealth is not a sacrifice. That is a destruction of freedom that we are experiencing. The sacrifice you and I know is unheard of in the policies that are now forced upon us.

When the government is in charge of GM now—even though they say they are not—things are really changing. When the government says the warranties are more secure now than ever, I took that as a slap in the face to our dealerships across our nation, that everything is okay now. Oh really? I want the old America back. This new

❧

American power grab is totally destroying our country. If you really listen to the techniques and strategies of our government, it is all a line for you to bow down and do what they say.

This movement is going against the Constitution and every right this country was built on. I think we need to take care of our own country, not tear it down private business by private business.

When the government starts firing people in private businesses, that isn't freedom. It's nationalization. When they tell you what to buy, sorry, that is not freedom. It's a step towards government stores. And when the big wheels start telling you that you cannot—brace yourself Texans—protect yourself or own a handgun or deer rifle, that sure the hell is not freedom.

A lot of Americans will agree with that last one. What about the smart car? Now that's a topic, isn't it? What farmer or rancher is going to plug in a box on wheels and charge the battery to pull a triple axel goose neck trailer full of bulls to the auction?

You have to remember folks, especially the youngsters out there, that you become what you think about most. That is so true. Our government thinks about crisis, crisis, and more crisis. Crisis is what they crave. Then after that they sit there and say it wasn't their fault. Imagine that, America.

Here is something to think about. Never, ever downgrade your level of intelligence or lifelong accomplishments just because someone does not have your success. Do not let the

୬

negativity pull you down and try to decrease your positive outlook. Keep being who you are. Keep building your way of life so others can learn from you. Stand out, be an individual model for people to look up to. Life would be boring if we were all the same, so don't tear down individuals that have a passion for life, and abundance for them (and others). Maybe life wouldn't be so damn hard if some people would just stop and think before they start the negativity game again.

Okay, just a couple more star points for our great administration.

- They need to stop playing the blame game and quit downing our country to other countries.

- We need to run America like it should be run. Why don't we worry about America for a change? If anyone wants to bow—and you all know who did—it should be the other countries bowing down to us and thanking America for the services and new freedoms we have provided for them.

We are not arrogant, we just happened to have paved the way for the rest of the world to enjoy a better life. Why do you think the USA has so many different cultures living here?

People come here for a reason, and that is to experience a prosperous and more abundant way of living. When our president goes overseas he now represents us, which means

જી

you and me. And what does he do, he does the exact opposite.

He should stand tall with authority. The world has learned from us, and he should have acted that way. And no, that is not being arrogant. That is simply being a leader of our country. Is that too much to ask? Apparently it is.

Dream big, America. Build the biggest damned business you can possibly build, and crush heedless government regulations. We will succeed. And America, it really does start with you. And I will be right beside you through it all.

Speaking of business, throwing money at ones that are going under is only pouring more fuel on the fire. Especially when we have bailouts, and stimulus packages that are building government and shrinking the private sector. If the money is not there, then it will not work. My nine-year-old can figure that out.

The firing of CEO's and other employees of a company by a president is not the answer. We have Chapters 11 or 13 in the U.S. Bankruptcy Code to take care of a failing business. We are Americans and we will start over if we have to. That is what we do.

We are too strong of a country to have the private sector be taken over by government. They will build you up and then your world comes crashing down and then on top of that, they blame no one else but the private business owner who is living the dream of a Free Individual American. Why is that? Our country was founded on the freedom to build your

৶

business the right way and be able to prosper. The right to Liberty, and the pursuit of happiness. Is that too hard to understand, Uncle Sam?

As the days go by, more and more peoples' lives are changing. There is that word again. Change this, and change that. It is one thing to change up a system for everyone. It is another when it is only so a government can control innocent people.

My heart breaks when I see all of this destruction going on in America. One company is shutting down on the east coast and then another out west. A bailout here and a bailout there. None of this seems to bother Washington. In any event, somebody is filling their pockets right now and it isn't the People.

Auto dealers all across the country were getting letters saying they had to shut their doors. What I don't understand is, why does a profitable business have to shut their doors? I mean, one of the main purposes of building a business is to make a profit and enjoy the fruits of your labor. And at the same time help your community out by providing a service to everyone.

Oh, I forgot, this new power grab we have now doesn't allow honest people and hard working people to benefit from their hard work. Work that they have been doing for years. And profits for the individual are off the table because you are now considered to be too greedy if you are a success. If only

ع

the big wheels would have looked in the mirror some years ago, we would not be in the position we are in.

Greed got the best of them. Big banks, credit card companies, and insurance companies. Fannie Mae and Freddie Mac, too. And after some bailouts, the bankers took the money and ran with it. Now the banks have the taxpayers' money and they won't even lend it out. Boy, that got the economy stimulated, didn't it?

It boils down to the little man versus the big man. The little man works his butt off while the big man's gets bigger and flabbier! He gets greedy and the money gets in the way of his doing the right thing.

Money is good, but sometimes money will destroy you. Money will make you lose sight of what is really important. And right now, our country is caught between survival and pure greed. Both sides of the aisle are just plain not working for America. Republicans and Democrats have both lost their way. Yes, I realize that there are some who are okay, but very few.

We cannot just bail out this company and bail out that one because the government doesn't have any money to do it. They are living in fantasy land, while we live in the real world. The government cannot save the day. To the people who have not realized this yet, I repeat: The Government Will Not Save The Day. They are in this for themselves. They will not tell you that, but they are.

The Working Man Fights for Right

୬

Look at your bank account and then take a peek at theirs. My little light comes on at the bank saying my account is almost empty. And at the same time, the money I had is being redistributed to people that do not know the meaning of that four-letter-word: WORK.

Look, I don't mean to depress you. We will get through this chapter together. The government will tell you that you will still be able to build this and build that, but you have to take into account that the hand and brains of Obama will be lurking in the shadows to shut you down if you don't run that business like the government wants you to. That is the difference. No more Freedom to run it like you want to. So the end result is they are looking for you to make a mistake, because they will be imbedded in your business as these takeovers keep coming as the months pass.

Man, life is good today at The White House. The plan by design to finish off the private sector and spread the wealth is shamelessly underway. Remember, we cannot let a crisis go to waste and, believe me, they are not wasting it. My whole life is going to waste because I am being forced to do things I don't want to do, but as long as our politicians keep getting richer and the Working Man keeps getting poorer, then I guess that it's Mission Accomplished for Washington.

We cannot go on like this. We are doing what we can to stay afloat and in spite of it all, some are still doing pretty good. When we call our congressman, we get the cold shoulder and become frustrated to no end.

❦

When we attend certain gatherings, we can clearly see that things just aren't working out for the average American who knows what it feels like to earn an honest living. This unbridled government takeover is spreading pretty fast. I don't think Washington knows what they are doing... They are just doing. A stimulus package will not bear fruit until a few years down the road. Our politicians cannot risk the true effects of it now because they will be long out of office by then.

The real estate market is steadily going south and the rentals are steadily slowing too. If you have no jobs, then you have no rental income. If the banks won't lend you the money that they were supposed to then no one will buy houses either. Slowly people will not want to invest in their own business because they know that government will eventually get it all anyway.

Do you see a trend here? Do you see a serious downturn in our America as government keeps expanding? This was once a country where you could be as big as you wanted to be.

This was a country where one man could not slow another man down. If you wanted to work twelve hours a day you could. If you wanted to work four hours a day you could do that too. Now everyone is forced to be on the same level and it doesn't matter how good you were before, or how rich you got from your own good decision making. You will be forced to be poor. What did I say? Yes, this new era of spreading the wealth is making the Working Man poor. The people who

The Working Man Fights for Right

ℒ

make this country work are being eliminated from the world of small business and are being punished for their hard work in the process.

We cannot be silenced anymore. We have to be vocal and be firm about it. When we go out into the world and protest against these endless programs that are being shoved down our throats, we have to let our new government know we will not tolerate this kind of blatant dishonesty against the people. Never think you will not make a difference. Each time you let your voice be heard that tells our leaders that we know that we're on to them. We are finding out who they really are and they know that, too.

Detroit will be back, better than ever one day (just as long as they don't push out baby Smart Cars every day). Farmers need more power than that to haul hay or pull auger buggies during harvest. The Smart Car isn't such a smart car to be in going down Interstate 10 through Houston, Texas during rush hour. That car looks like an ant compared to an eighteen wheeler. I am still trying to figure out where to put my goose neck hitch on that Smart Car. I mean, if that is all we are going to be driving to save the planet I need to think ahead, right?

I personally love the smell and the smoke of a diesel engine winding down the highway in the middle of the day. Our big trucks haven't been totally shut down yet, but we are hurting. Like I said, everything is going according to plan.

A greener environment won't save the world either. I mean, what more does our government want? My grass is

❧

green in my front yard. Just because the ozone is hardly ever changing, our government thinks they can fix that too. The winters are still pretty damn cold and our summers couldn't get any hotter. So go figure. Shutting down particular businesses to save the planet is not going to save the planet.

Taxing everyone to death to add another false program is not the answer either. All of this is meant to build this government bigger and bigger while we're being lied to in the process.

From health care issues, our personal business on our computers, to the amount of fuel we put into our cars and trucks, how are we supposed to live under this new government? What do they want us to do?

America is going through some changes and let me tell you, I am trying to hang on. We have to stay focused on our beliefs and our true inner selves. I know it feels like the walls are caving in on you and around you but we, as Americans who still love the freedom to live our own lives, have to let others know that we will get through this no matter what.

We, as Americans, will prevail. Let's turn this country around the way the people can. Continue to work hard in spite of Big Government and we will be America once again.

CHAPTER 11

That's What I Like About Texas!

As you can see, I am a Texan. I love it, and would not change that at all. We Texans are known as a bunch of rednecks or backwoods boys. That's fine, because you know why? Because some of us are.

Why change who you are? We like a number of things down South and so here are a few salesman items for you America, in case you want to visit us one day. The difference

இ

in the government and my thoughts are this. I am telling you the truth about my issues and topics.

We like big things down here, and I won't go into detail, but you'll get the picture. We are people who like to ride around town, about four feet off the ground in a pickup truck. Or let's just say in a vehicle almost high enough to walk under.

We duel our trucks out and rattle pipes between the businesses and the courthouse on Main Street. We like riding around with our girlfriends sitting right smack dab beside us. She is so close to me that the cops think I have two heads. They just wave and let me drive right on by.

In Texas you can drive down your streets and just about anybody will stop and give you a wave.

I like a cold beer at the end of the day. I like to go down to the ocean, down around Rock Port, and throw out a line and see if I can catch a red fish or a trout. Sometimes I catch hard head catfish. They say birds of a feather flock together, maybe there is some truth to that. Sometimes I am one. A hard head that is. Just relaxing at the beach or sitting on the balcony down at South Padre Island or Corpus Christi.

I put my big behind in the water and my toes in the sand, along with a Crown and Coke, wondering when I can have my next beer summit. Life is good isn't it?

Down here we talk a little different and I like that because Texans are different. Diju eatjet? Or... arrite, I tell you what.

The Working Man Fights for Right

§

Some say y'all and ya'hear. That's a biggin'. I was first, what abouchew? Just to name a few.

If you're a Texan you can speak the language. If you would like to learn this language, just come on down here and we can teacha, without taxing everyone for the classes. We also say, "mornin'" instead of good morning. And one more. We say howdy and yes ma'am and no ma'am, yes sir and no sir. And I like a good ol' brewsky in one hand.

Texas also is known for her rivers and lakes. There ain't nothing like sitting at the lake and just kicking back with a cold beverage. Or maybe running a trout line in the Guadalupe River. I also like honkytonks on Saturday nights. I like slow dancing with my beautiful wife. Or taking her for a ride across our pasture on our four-wheeler. Down here in the great state of Texas we have plenty of land and spacious skies to enjoy.

Texas is home to some of the largest rodeos in the world and some of the best bull riding you will ever see. We also have trophy exotics, such as axis, fallow, and black buck antelope.

We have beautiful mountains, and the hill country is also a sight to see. Our barbeque will satisfy your hunger and we won't care if the sauce is running down your chin either. We have miles of high fences and plenty of low ones, which means shovel-ready jobs are a common thing down here. We have so much job creation and prosperity and desire to build businesses that we don't even have to tax anyone or anything to get the job started or finished. I might add just one thing. Remember the old saying, All hat and no cattle? Well I've got one for you. The new America we are in is, All politics and no common sense!

Texas is the home of the *Dallas Cowboys* and *Houston Texans*. From the *San Antonio Spurs* to the *Dallas Mavericks*, or even the *Houston Astros, Dynamos*, and the *Houston Rockets*, we have it all.

The Alamo and the River Walk are great sights also. Texas is a great place to live and a great place to work. Oil companies, on shore to off shore jobs, we have them all.

The Mexican food is great, too. You can live on that alone. Whatever tickles your fancy, Texas is a wonderful place to live and raise a family. I fly our Texas Flag proudly. We live in one of the best places you could ever imagine. From the coastline to the hill country. You can either hunt trophy exotics or trophy whitetails. Whatever you want to do Texas has it. Great schools and colleges? Go visit Austin.

And don't forget your guitar. Some of the world's best music comes out of Austin. From the cotton fields to the corn fields.

We don't hesitate to help anyone either. If it is a storm or just a flat tire, we are there for one another. We don't wait on the government before we make a move. We are almost finished with the task before the government knows what's going on. If you think about it, Texas has just about anything and everything you need to survive, to live, to have a good time, and it's a great spot to go on vacation.

You know what else? I would just have to say Texas is like a whole other country. We are people who actually use our own brains for our own success. Texans build each other up, not tear everyone down in order to see progress. The list goes on and on doesn't it? One more thing: Don't Mess With Texas, and most of all, God Bless Texas.

CHAPTER 12

Guns In America

I have a right to bear arms and to protect myself. And now we have yet another assault on another freedom we have in this country. Why is that? They just can't leave well enough alone. Why can't we protect ourselves without the government getting involved? What is wrong with owning a gun? What is wrong with buying another one? The gun does not kill, people do. In this society we really do have to consider some kind of self defense and be safe.

The Working Man Fights for Right

ॐ

There are some who will hurt people and don't care about anybody. And then there are some who will go through life trying to do good. Some keep a clean record and are able to buy a gun and some don't. Others prefer handguns over rifles. Some will carry without permits. Concealed hand gun licenses would be wise, but nowadays a lot of people don't care. It is always better safe than sorry.

People these days are scared about the gun laws and the future regulations we may be facing. Why we have to change everything, don't ask me.

Americans will do anything in their power to protect their families. We will do what it takes to protect ourselves also. Now this does not always have to lead to guns, but since we are on the subject we will keep it our main focus. When guns get into the wrong hands, we've got trouble.

There is always somebody in the crosshairs of a gun and unfortunately some are fatal during a robbery or gang violence or maybe even in our schools. We have a fight on our hands in Texas with the borders and such and it is not getting any better.

When you hear about all the violence, many people think we should get rid of all of the guns—that they are bad. Not necessarily. If you get rid of all the guns, some people who needed one will now not have one. We don't want that, do we?

America knows that Texas has plenty of guns. With all of the deer running around, why not? A man's gotta eat, doesn't

≈

he? A lot of people don't realize what it really feels like to own a gun. Once they see one, there are some that are scared of them, and that's okay. If you are scared of one, then leave it alone. Or you can take some training and will maybe feel more comfortable about handling one. It is your free choice to do so if you please.

Of course, if you try to buy one you will have to have a background check done on you. Right there stops the honest ones from owning one (Even though they can still buy one from a friend). They went ahead with a background check anyway.

If the government insists on more regulations, we will be left with tumble weeds in the streets and John Wayne-types looking down a double barrel shotgun at us. I'll have to go to the small town saloon and get me a shot of whiskey before we head out on the trail again. And in the morning, I'll go into the river with my little screen and pan and look for gold nuggets.

My dollar will be so far gone, gold panning is all I'll have left. Instead of being the Lone Ranger, I will be the lone stranger. What would people do if we went back into the old days? Texans will be fine. We live off the land and we would survive. We know how to go out and harvest a ten point whitetail buck, or go under banking in a river for a big old yellow catfish.

We are country folks down here. Our guns are almost like the ball point pens that we carry around. When you go check the pasture you watch out for snakes and look for coyotes getting in along the fence lines. So having a gun is not all bad for everyone.

If you have any common sense you will be fine. Our lives are to be lived in freedom and the peace of mind to do whatever we want to do within the boundaries of the state laws and federal laws.

Why does the government threaten to take guns from the individuals of this country? The good guys mean no harm with firearms, but are being targeted again. It would be nice if our leaders would go after the people corrupting our society instead of those who mind their own business.

Whenever you get a chance to take a youngster deer hunting, do it. There is nothing better than to see your son or daughter shoot their first buck or doe. Were we hurting anything? No. Did we put food on the table? Yes.

We hunted during whitetail season, and tagged the dear properly and quartered it up in a reasonable manner and came home. We took a few pictures for happy memories and called it a day. So what is the problem with me owning a deer rifle in America? Not a damned thing.

A handgun is a little more dangerous because it is so small and can be hidden. Everyone is buying them now and buying more ammo. Our government is scaring the daylights out of people. Can't they see what is going on? People are scared and nervous about everything. They want this country to be safer and more civilized, but it is turning out to be the exact opposite. The owners at your gun stores and retail stores are struggling to keep ammo in stock.

The government can't talk about gun stores suffering; man, are they are prospering. Like I said, government loves a good crisis. What better way to have one than to take away our right to bear arms. This list goes on and on. If the people cannot have guns, then our politicians shouldn't need them either.

Our freedoms are slowly being taken from us day by day. We have to wake people up and let them know what is really going on. Washington has so many ways of talking to and manipulating us, it is quite unbelievable. They say what you want to hear and not what you really need to hear. And at the same time they are just saving themselves and are not worried about the people who believed in them.

Let me put it this way, Uncle Sam. My gun is *my gun*. My property is *my property*. I worked to earn money and to buy what I want to buy. If I choose to buy a handgun, I will. If I choose to buy a shotgun or rifle, I will. Try tracking down the people who are stealing them and do what you want to them for a change. Leave the good guys alone.

Don't give me a speech about guns and gun control. We have enough control over us already. My purchase of a weapon is my free choice and my decision. If I want to go quail hunting, I will. (Under one condition. I will not hunt next to former Vice President Cheney.) I don't need to be peppered by BBs.

The Working Man Fights for Right

୭

Some people go through life, never training or really learning how to use a firearm. I encourage you to do so. Just be safe and be aware of your surroundings. Always watch yourself, Always. The freedom to keep our guns will be another fight for the people. We know what is going on already. We know that having the freedom to own a gun is a great privilege to have. So why mess with us about it? Why all the worrying about the individual owning a gun?

If you want our weapons, then this is what will happen. There will be people with guns that you have missed. Some may even be bad guys. There will be an over population of deer, hogs, and especially the exotic species that enhances Texas's visibility to the rest of the nation.

The rattlesnakes, copperheads, and many others will be crawling up your pant leg when you are sleeping. Try telling this to all of the outdoorsmen across the nation. I guess we will have to use our knives to kill the cattle at the meat packing places, because you won't be able to use a gun their either.

We will be invaded by the popular bird, called the dove, because our shotguns will be confiscated too. Is this making anyone mad yet? What is Uncle Sam going to do when all of our vehicles are damaged while we drive down the highways across the country and get hit from all of the wildlife?

We can tell Uncle Sam, "Well, we did have management programs to control deer populations and we increased the

❧

buck to doe ratio pretty significantly. But since this happened, I guess we will have to have another government program."

If our guns are taken away then all of this has a domino effect on society or let's say a major backlash to us all. I don't think Washington realizes this.

On a more serious note, the people are scared, nervous, and furious that our gun rights are now in jeopardy. It is bad enough for people to be losing their jobs and their retirement plans. This will only create more violence, because we are living in troubled times. Some people are getting desperate, and they are getting to where they don't care who they hurt.

With money getting tighter every day, we really have to protect ourselves more than ever now. It is harder to trust people and to live under a controlled environment, much less lose the second amendment.

I advise you that if you do have a gun, keep it away from your kids. If it is visible, teach them about it. Teach gun safety. Teach them that this is just for hunting or just for protection when necessary. We all hope that we never have to shoot anyone in a self defense situation.

The bottom line is this... Study your amendments. Be aware of what they are and what they mean for you, the free American. We cannot afford, as a free nation, to lose anymore freedoms. We have to be able to protect ourselves. Our police forces understand this fully. Like I said before. Go get your Concealed Handgun License. The police force in your area will appreciate it greatly. You will then have taken a step towards doing the right thing. If you want to carry a handgun, then do it the right way. Do things the right way and you will live a more calm and peaceful life.

One more thing. Fight to keep the right to bear arms here in America because, I will tell you once again, don't think for a second that the government forgot about you. They are making their way through every privilege and right we have as free individuals.

Protect yourself. Remember that the government does not have all the answers for you. They just have all of your money. Practice gun safety and take a child hunting.

CHAPTER 13

Old Glory

Has our flag lost its meaning? Does it have to be such a big deal just to hoist it on a flag pole and be proud of our country and the property she flies above, wherever that maybe? Things are getting ridiculous, even with flying our true symbol of freedom.

The Working Man Fights for Right

๑

The flag has a history of achievement and accomplishment about our country.

Our own people are finding out that we cannot even fly it in our front yards or in certain communities. I welcome all cultures to come to America the right way and have a chance to grab a little freedom or prosperity here, but I am going to tell you like it is.

If America is getting to the point where certain people are getting offended because Old Glory is flying above the subdivision they are living in, I have six words for you: Go back where you came from. You are now on American soil, it's called The United States of America. You wanted freedom. Well, flying our country's flag is one of those freedoms. If you are an American citizen, get over it. Is this our final days of a free America?

Where is our common sense anymore? We have to stop these rules and regulations that are interfering with our everyday lives, like simply flying the flag in our yards. Our freedoms are not are freedoms anymore. We cannot stand for this. We have had enough. We cannot allow yet another flaw in our society to become evident. Corruption of our country is crawling across the land and if this keeps up, wait another six months or a year. The people are enraged with this power grab and we aren't going back to sleep. The betrayal of the American individual has awakened us, and we are not backing down. We may not sleep ever again.

∝

Let me throw this at you. The government owns about 30 percent of our private sector and wealth. If Obama's health care plan is added in, then it will be another 18 percent. After the climate bill this will add another 8 percent. Do you want 56 percent of your freedoms controlled by our government? Well, it is coming.

What happened to *our* America? Geed, Greed, Greed. Our leaders have unleashed their power on the innocent people of this great land. Now it is our turn to give them and others that are government officials that are not for freedom for the individual a one-way ticket out of Washington.

One day it is a fish. One day we are not supposed to fly our flag. And the next day it is the invasion of privacy in our lives. One day someone brings up the fear of owning a gun and the next day we have global warming, something that most people could not care less about. Even though we are still having some pretty cold winters, and in some parts of the country winter storms started earlier than usual, it seems to me that God may be playing a major role in all of this weather stuff. I mean, he did create everything. And ultimately, God does have the last word. God will decide what needs to happen in the end.

I will fly my flag above my property and my land. I am an American and nothing or nobody will ever change that. People need to wake up and realize that there is more going on around us than you really think. I mean, I know we are all working hard and have busy lives, but never lose sight of where your country—the one that you truly love—is now going. Pull your head out of the sand and sit up and shake it off.

Clear your mind from the rat race you are in. Whatever the situation, just wake up and be aware. Your country depends on the adults, and your kids depend on you. We have to continue to stay focused on where we are going in life. I cannot stress this enough.

Don't get tired on me. This fight has just begun. The American individual will turn the tables on this government take over and I will call it Operation Individual Freedom.

We cannot let these regulations control us. United We Stand, whether it is abroad or here at home. The fight for freedom has really come home this time.

As I drive the Texas highways, I see more and more U.S. Flags flying high above businesses, ranches, homes, and also painted on the sides of barns and sheds, too. Those people aren't bothering anyone. They are simply showing their respect and honor for their country. More people need to fly the flag and be proud of their country. There isn't anything better than to see Old Glory flying above someone's property as you are driving down the highway. It's a property where the family that lives there has worked hard to get it to look the way it does. And then they put the last finishing touches on their property with an American flag flying high above for all the world to see. Now that is America to me.

CHAPTER 14

Speak Out!

Why are things so complicated in America? Why are things so difficult? Why do people destroy other peoples' dreams and never miss a beat? Why is it that one person thinks they can control a whole group of people, even when some disagree? Ask yourself these questions and think about them. Why can't we all just get along? Why does a politician build up people, just to let them down? Why do the people have to put up with a politician who does not care about them? How can a president at any given time not send help to our soldiers in need and still sleep at night? I would like that one to be answered right now

I am curious. How can a soccer mom survive this kind of atmosphere? How can a doctor do his job to the fullest when he or she has so many regulations, issues, and laws to abide by, just to help one single patient in need?

Why is it that when we were supposed to have been freed from all the pain that our America we live in now feels like a foreign country?

These are some really funny questions aren't they? I have some more.

Why does someone that supposedly loves freedom want to stick their nose into everyone's business and restrict them from doing what they want to do, and need to do, to run a successful business?

Why are we called hate mongers, but love America for who she is? Why are the people who are keeping this country going being punished? Why are the people who are controlling this country—not running it, but controlling it—still in power? Why do We The People have to put up with this? The fact of the matter is, we don't. Why? Because we are Americans.

We are the builders, we are the veins, the arteries, the blood that flows through each state across this country. We keep this country afloat. Without the Working Man there

The Working Man Fights for Right

would be no America, there would be no economy, there would be no military.

So why ask why when our own government will not listen to us? It is time the individual takes charge of our country. And the time is now! And at the end of the day, who will you turn to for answers? God.

Always keep God first and pray for this country and stay close to the ones you love the most. Your family will stick with you through it all, remember that. Enjoy your kids each and every day. Allow them to be kids. They love it when daddy or mommy acts like a kid with them. That will bring you closer together more than ever before .

I hope you will be a more positive person after reading my thoughts. We are living in a different world now. Some say big government is the answer while others believe that smaller government is the answer. Whatever the case may be we have to stick together through it all.

I pray every day that our country stays free. I pray every day that we always be the country we were two-hundred-thirty-seven years ago. Our founding fathers built this free country for all of mankind to enjoy and not let it get torn down by big government or laziness.

A lot of people have worked really hard to provide for their children and themselves. The working class people know what I am talking about. The entrepreneurs know what I am talking about also. Our service men and women really know what I am talking about. The ultimate sacrifice is the fight for freedom. Do you know why? Because now we are worried, scared, angry, and depressed. Our world is changing right before our eyes. Some find it hard to believe and some just could not care less.

The truth is that I am really scared and worried about my America that I knew just a short time ago. A man doesn't always have to hide his tears when he really feels strong about a subject. That man is me. I have a job to do and I will do it for the sake of my wife and kids. Do any of you feel the same way out there? I know you do. We are in this together.

Remember this: What goes up must come down. And right now our America is going down from the inside out. So with that being said. There is no other way for us to go. Our only way is up. Our nation is on a downslide on the road to nowhere. So whoever loves freedom, let's join together and start heading upward. Remember, the sky's the limit. Our country is waiting for us to take her back.

You always have to remember, every morning when you wake up, that you are in the best country in the whole world. We will have some troubled times ahead, but we will succeed. We will each experience more stressed-out days than you can imagine. We will have a number of weeks when we are short on cash. But always remember that you will still get through those hard times because God is on your side.

The Working Man Fights for Right

So take your expertise and go for your dreams. Don't let anyone get in your way. This is America and this is the place for you to become the person you have always wanted to be.

Whatever you do out there is your business and the individual freedoms will not ever be taken away from us. Our freedoms are fragile, and we are here to save it. Speak out; please, speak out!. Your money is your money, remember that. And once the people stop giving the government money, then the government will think again. The government will wonder what happened.

I am writing this as I am on the road and I am now going to go see my wonderful wife and kids at home. After all, they are the reason I do what I do—and love what I do—because if anybody deserves the best in life, it is my family.

I will continue to drive the beautiful Texas highways through the good days and the not-so-good. Stay positive about your life and never get sidetracked. Always remember that *The road goes on forever and the party never ends.*

God Bless you, God Bless our president, and remember this when you gather together to pray as a family tonight. Put aside all of the anger and jokes and ask God to give our president the strength and courage to pull this country out of this mess and to protect our president no matter what.

Allow God to come into your lives and forever prosper. Now my cell phone is ringing again, I'll talk to you later, I gotta go.

ABOUT THE AUTHOR

Author Scott Jeffrey Filip is the quintessential ordinary man. Hailing from south Texas, this man in the black hat, the boots, and sometimes camouflage, is a guy who minds his own business and just tries to put food on the table for his family.

He praises God, loves the outdoors, and loves the state of Texas. He has no hesitation when it comes to helping people out and he believes that receiving a thank you or a hug, or maybe a simple hand shake, is worth more than a paycheck.

This is Scott's America, but he feels it is shrinking away in a mire of political chicanery, selfishness, and a thieving redistribution of wealth that has all but destroyed the middle class.

"We live in the best country in the world. God created America and now it is up to us to maintain it as a wealthy nation," Scott says. "Keep God first in your life and you will be the person you never thought you would be, and from that simple act our country will rise again."

www.ingramcontent.com/pod-product-compliance
Lightning Source LLC
Chambersburg PA
CBHW020509290526
45786CB00002B/531